Leading Professional Conversations

Adaptive expertise for schools

HELEN TIMPERLEY

Published in 2025 by Amba Press, Melbourne, Australia
www.ambapress.com.au

First published in 2023 by ACER Press, an imprint of
Australian Council for Educational Research Ltd

© Helen Timperley 2025

In the spirit of reconciliation, Amba Press acknowledges the Traditional Custodians of Country throughout Australia and their connections to land, sea and community. We pay our respect to their elders past and present and extend that respect to all Aboriginal and Torres Strait Islander peoples today.

This book is copyright. All rights reserved. Except under the conditions described in the *Copyright Act 1968* of Australia and subsequent amendments, and any exceptions permitted under the current statutory licence scheme administered by Copyright Agency (www.copyright.com.au), no part of this publication may be reproduced, stored in a retrieval system, transmitted, broadcast or communicated in any form or by any means, optical, digital, electronic, mechanical, photocopying, recording or otherwise, without the written permission of the publisher.

This work was initially commissioned by the Victorian Department of Education. ACER Press was grateful for the DET's permission to publish the work.

Edited by Shaneen Goodwin
Cover design, text design and typesetting by Karen Wilson

ISBN: 9781923569324 (pbk)
ISBN: 9781923569331 (ebk)

A catalogue record for this book is available from the National Library of Australia.

Foreword

What a relief to know we can now draw on Helen Timperley's most recent thinking about professional learning conversations to inform our change work!

Professor Timperley's previous research outlining what constitutes powerful professional learning has helped many educators globally. Developing adaptive expertise is essential if we are to address the complex challenges of equity and quality for all learners. Helen has taught us that adaptive expertise is developed through collaborative inquiry and professional conversations. We fully accept that argument and feel privileged to have worked with Helen to develop the *Spiral of inquiry*, which asks educators to be curious about what is going on for their learners and to engage in a disciplined inquiry process to improve those experiences.

Now, in *Leading professional conversations*, Helen provides the tools for leading conversations that will grow adaptive expertise in a complex educational environment.

Helen's deep scholarship and respect for practice is visible on every page. Her appreciation for the wise use of time in advancing adult learning is insightful. The detail of her suggested frameworks based on years of experience in helping adults learn is important. This book is both conceptually strong and practical. All learners – adults and young people – will benefit from the use of its considered strategies.

Helen takes us from the skills needed to get started in purposeful conversations to the use of artefacts through to the expert level where we learn to resolve disagreements, develop metacognition and check for unconscious bias. Educators who apply these approaches will be able to lead short, informed, focused and fruitful professional conversations.

Teachers will value the useful and respectful ideas about using short videos (rather than supervisory 'visits') in their learning processes. Wise leaders will form partnerships to plan and practise their skills so they can master authentic inquiry. Thoughtful system leaders will use ideas in the book to create inquiry-oriented learning cultures.

What brings these ideas to life are the conversations Helen uses to illustrate key points. These transcripts address the complex challenges faced by educators regardless of their position. As former principals and district leaders, we see ourselves reflected in many of the conversations. The strategies in this book for planning and analysing conversations are invaluable. We only wish we had had this resource when we were leading schools.

We are working in a time where ideas that help us build stronger democratic practices into our work are vital. Educators who work together to help others think evaluatively, to listen to diverse perspectives and to seek deep knowledge as they grapple with how to make more of a difference are creating much more inclusive cultures.

From the outset, Helen Timperley's work has been about making a difference to the young people we serve in our schools. Her scholarship about professional learning has influenced our thinking and actions for years. This book takes us to a deeper understanding about how to have intentional, focused conversations that will build the expertise educators need, and young people deserve.

Leading professional conversations is a superb gift to our profession.

Judy Halbert and **Linda Kaser**
Co-Directors Networks of Inquiry and Indigenous Education Lead Faculty, Transformative Educational Leadership Program, University of British Columbia

Contents

Foreword	iii
Acknowledgements	vii

CHAPTER 1
Conversations, complex challenges and adaptive expertise — 1

Introduction	1
Educational challenges and the expertise required	2
Attributes of adaptive expertise	8
Conversations to develop adaptive expertise	12
Outline of the book	17

CHAPTER 2
Getting started — 21

Introduction	21
Establish the purpose and focus	21
Evidence and artefacts	24
Engage beliefs	30
Build actionable knowledge	33
Genuine inquiry	36
Plan professional conversations	41
Analyse your conversations	43

CHAPTER 3
Going deeper — 47

Introduction	47
Build theoretical knowledge through practice	47
Ladder of inference	52
Unpack theories of practice	58

Agree on the problem before the solution 65
Acknowledge emotion and vulnerability 68
Plan and analyse deeper conversations 71

CHAPTER 4
Expert level 73

Introduction 73
Co-construct conversations 74
Promote self-regulated learning 77
Develop self-awareness: metacognition 79
Keep the main thing the main thing 81
Resolve disagreements 83
Check unconscious bias and equity 85
Professional learning conversations in teams 87
Plan and analyse expert conversations 89

CHAPTER 5
Observation and analysis of practice 91

Introduction 91
Phase 1: pre-observation conversation 93
Phase 2: protocols for observation/video recording 100
Phase 3: co-constructed analysis of practice 102
Phase 4: co-constructed new practice 105
Observation and analysis: further thoughts 108

CHAPTER 6
Bringing it all together 111

Supplementary digital resources 116

References 117

Acknowledgements

I want to acknowledge the many educators who have engaged with earlier versions of this book. They demonstrated high levels of adaptive expertise as they analysed their professional conversations and set new professional learning goals, together with providing feedback about how to make the material in the book more accessible. I would also like to thank Dr Kaye Twyford specifically for the many conversations we have had to improve the clarity and focus of this book.

CHAPTER 1
Conversations, complex challenges and adaptive expertise

Introduction

Expectations of educators at every level of the system have grown exponentially over the last few years. Students have more diverse needs as their circumstances have become increasingly complex. Teachers need support to meet these needs but are likely to have very different beliefs about how leaders should engage with teachers. Leaders are also expected to meet growing state and national agendas for schooling. Yet at its heart, schooling is still about educating students and caring for their wellbeing. The leadership actions with most impact on educational, social and emotional outcomes for students are those that address the pedagogical core (Elmore 2004; Robinson et al. 2008). This kind of leadership has various labels, such as pedagogical leadership, instructional leadership or leadership for learning (Timperley and Robertson 2011).

The essence of pedagogical leadership involves system and school leaders actively leading the professional learning of other educators in their schools in ways that enhance outcomes for each student in their care. Much has been written on the desirability of this approach to leadership but much less about the specifics of putting it into practice. Pedagogical leadership is primarily exercised through professional conversations, supported by relevant evidence and appropriate artefacts (forms of evidence and other elements used to illustrate educational practices). These conversations are pivotal in translating more formal knowledge about effectiveness into every teaching and learning environment in every school, every day.

This book is designed to support leaders to have these kinds of professional learning conversations. It is intended for anyone in a leadership position who is responsible for promoting the professional learning of others. Sometimes the conversations involve only one other person, at other times it may be a whole staff or a group of other leaders, such as team leaders or faculty heads.

The central question addressed in this book:

> As a leader, how can I promote the professional learning of those educators for whom I have responsibility and their ability to improve their professional practice in ways that enhance outcomes for students?

This book does not specifically focus on addressing issues of professional competence or underperformance. Different kinds of conversations are needed for these purposes. It does address issues around disagreements and vulnerabilities when these arise in the course of a professional learning conversation.

In this chapter, I begin by highlighting key features of the kinds of challenges educators face in their everyday work that require new professional learning, then describe the key attributes of professional expertise needed to address these challenges. Finally, I outline the qualities of professional conversations that together enhance professional learning in ways that develop adaptive expertise. Subsequent chapters describe the specifics of these conversations, illustrated with examples from a range of school and system roles.

Professional time is one of the most valuable resources in education. Many educators feel overworked with not enough time to do everything. However, the time taken for professional conversations is unrelated to the extent to which these conversations promote learning (Timperley 2011). Long conversations are often long because they are unfocused. The conversations outlined in this book are about maximising time to promote the kind of deep professional learning that results in changes to practice and improved student outcomes, particularly those relating to equity and inclusion. Being clear about expectations, negotiating the focus and criteria for an observation and jointly deciding what evidence is relevant all save time while deepening educational knowledge and changing practice.

Educational challenges and the expertise required

How educational challenges are framed, and how they are addressed, are underpinned by assumptions about the professional expertise required for sustainable impact. This section elaborates the differences between simple, complicated and complex challenges or problems (Heifetz et al. 2009; Margolis and Strom 2020; Opfer and Pedder 2011; Snyder 2013).

It then considers the kinds of expertise that need to be developed through professional conversations.

Simple problems can be solved through a formula that can be repeated with relatively little expertise. Predictable results are expected. Few problems faced by teachers or leaders are of this nature so I will not address them further.

Complicated problems require higher order expertise, but their defining features are that effective solutions are known and can be taught. Once learned, reasonably predictable results can be expected. The different parts add up to the whole, so each part can be analysed and learned separately, then combined into a solution. These kinds of problems are sometimes referred to as technical (Heifetz et al. 2009). Examples of complicated problems might be a teacher setting up a class at the beginning of the year in ways that develop positive relationships and clear expectations. There are well established routines for this kind of situation. For a leader, it might involve learning to enter a budget into a computer program or writing policies for student safety. The development of routine expertise is essential to address these challenges. All educational organisations need effective routines, and the relevant expertise, in order to function well.

Routine expertise is efficient when problems are clearly defined and there are known effective solutions that can be directly taught and implemented with support. Those with routine expertise have sufficient knowledge, often acquired through experience, to address these more technical challenges (Hatano and Inagaki 1986). They can act quickly and adjust their practice incrementally as circumstances change.

This kind of expertise is not sufficient, however, to address complex challenges that typically have multiple causes, and often persist despite everyone's best attempts to address them. Complex challenges, sometimes referred to as adaptive challenges (Heifetz 2010; Heifetz et al. 2009; Shaked and Schechter 2020), cannot be meaningfully dismantled into discrete parts because they are characterised by interactions and interdependencies (Cochran-Smith et al. 2014; Opfer and Pedder 2011; Timperley et al. 2020). The parts cannot be understood independently of the whole, nor are cause and effect clearly linked. Rather, things spiral, sometimes with unexpected consequences. For example, teachers may become aware that the usual routines to set expectations and relationships at the beginning of the year are actually alienating for some students. The cultural practices of these students are not embraced, their home language is unintentionally dismissed as unimportant, and they quickly disengage. A few words of welcome in a home language are rarely sufficient to re-engage these students. Rather, much deeper inquiry is needed about the differences between teachers' and the students' cultural assumptions, the subtleties and signals given to the students about what is important, and appropriate ways to interact. These issues also apply at a whole-school level. The challenge then becomes how to establish early routines in classrooms and schools in ways that engage not only these students, but also include the learning and wellbeing of others.

These complex challenges are essentially about interactions and interdependencies; they have multiple causes with contested solutions. Continuing to address them using previous strategies can create ongoing dysfunction that is often not recognised. The challenges become noticeable when different stakeholders have different perspectives and when previous efforts to address them have not been as effective as hoped.

Complex challenges require adaptive expertise to address them. In education, adaptive expertise sees leaders and teachers using their deep educational knowledge to respond in the moment to accelerate student learning and improve their wellbeing. It demands in-depth educational knowledge and skills that are employed flexibly and responsively, rather than subscribing to preconceived ideas about what effective leadership and teaching should look like irrespective of context (Le Fevre et al. 2020). Figure 1.1 outlines the key features of complex challenges that require adaptive expertise to address them. It also identifies why it is important to recognise these challenges and how to do so. In the bottom right-hand quadrant, the essential features of professional conversations that develop adaptive expertise are also identified. These conversations require addressing issues holistically, engaging in causal inquiry and analysis while capturing multiple perspectives, acknowledging that change is emotionally charged, and seeking constant feedback about impact.

A defining feature of complex challenges is that they cannot be understood or addressed in 'pieces'. Rather, leaders need to shift between taking an overview, or seeing the whole (for example, 'What does our school stand for and what are our priorities?') while simultaneously examining the specific parts (for example, 'How is this group of students doing in relation to what our school stands for and its priorities?'). Heifetz et al. (2009) refer to this process as being both on the balcony for the wider view, and on the messiness of the dance floor in order to understand what is really happening. If the balcony view is focused on equity,

Complex challenges requiring adaptive expertise	
What are they? • They are challenges characterised by interactions and interdependencies so the pieces cannot be understood independently of the whole. • They usually have multiple causes, so it is difficult to identify what leads to what. • Solutions require a holistic approach that includes beliefs, values, experiences and identity. • Solutions are likely to be contested and may require new ways of thinking and acting. • Design and implementation become an ongoing process, with emerging evidence and its interpretation shaping the next phase.	**Why do they matter?** • Fixing a 'piece' (e.g. a specific teaching practice) fails to address the interactions and interdependencies of the whole. • If a single cause is acted on, then the problem is unlikely to be solved. • Solutions require more than just changing practice and must include the underlying beliefs that maintain that practice. • Continuing to solve complex problems using previous solutions can create ongoing dysfunction. • No amount of planning can anticipate all difficulties without embedded feedback loops to find out if things are improving.
How would I recognise them? • People have different opinions that sometimes focus on 'others' doing things differently rather than themselves ('everyone but me'). • Previous attempts to fix 'bits' of the problem (e.g. teaching practice) have not worked. • Different stakeholders have different perspectives about the causes. • When change is discussed, those involved may react emotionally. • Past attempts to solve them are not working. • Design and implementation are iterative, with implementation framed as learning opportunities.	**What kind of conversations address them?** • Conversations are focused on everyone's contributions ('everyone including me'). • Leaders talk about how the 'pieces' (e.g. teaching practice) are shaped by the school, and how the pieces contribute to the school as a whole. • Causal inquiry and analysis encourage multiple perspectives. • Vulnerability and emotion in the change process is acknowledged. • Past solutions are used as part of the problem identification and analysis process. • Questions of 'Did it work?' are replaced with 'Are we on track?'

FIGURE 1.1 Key attributes of complex challenges requiring adaptive expertise

for example, the details of the dance floor will involve examining closely which groups of students are not doing as well as others. Why these students and what is going on for them? It may also include a focus on their teachers, and lead to questions, such as 'Do these teachers have the knowledge and skills to engage with these students?', 'Is it an issue of beliefs and expectations?' or 'Why haven't these teachers embraced the new practices related to inclusion promoted in previous professional learning?'

It may mean asking questions about leadership that are closer to the balcony view. These sorts of questions might include 'Are these teachers receiving the right support from team leaders?' and 'Do these leaders see this as part of their role?' This back-and-forth view between the whole and the different parts is important because there are usually multiple issues that need to be addressed. The questions become an integral part of any professional conversation, whether with a leader or a teacher.

Yet most challenges in education are approached as if they are complicated rather than complex and as if developing routine expertise is sufficient to progress them. A 'piece' of practice is identified as in need of improvement and 'treated' as if that is sufficient (Le Fevre et al. 2020). If a leader, for example, needs to construct an annual improvement plan, many jurisdictions offer a template to identify separate priorities, as if they are operating independently of one another and from the history of previous improvement efforts, from the issues that led to those priorities being identified, and from the myriad of possible inter-dependent causes that are usually a mix of community, student, teacher, leader and organisational issues.

Similarly, improvements in teaching and learning are often treated as complicated. For example, if students' writing achievement is low, framing the problem as complicated typically involves a first step of leaders working with teachers to analyse what students know and need to know to improve their writing. Often this leads to resourcing a new writing program or bringing in an expert to engage teachers in professional development. The implied assumption underpinning this solution is that the teaching is inadequate, but this assumption is never explicitly stated or discussed. The next even shakier assumption is that the students' writing will improve. The cause of the problem and its solution are treated as essentially linear as shown in Figure 1.2.

Sometimes student achievement does improve in this scenario, but more often than not, gains are small and rarely sustained, because this linear reasoning belies the complexity of most student learning challenges. This linear thinking usually ignores community cultures; students' and teachers' beliefs, motivations and emotions; the culture of the school; and how the school leaders promote professional learning together with the nature of the associated conversations.

Conversations, complex challenges and adaptive expertise   7

FIGURE 1.2 Linear approaches to address complicated challenges

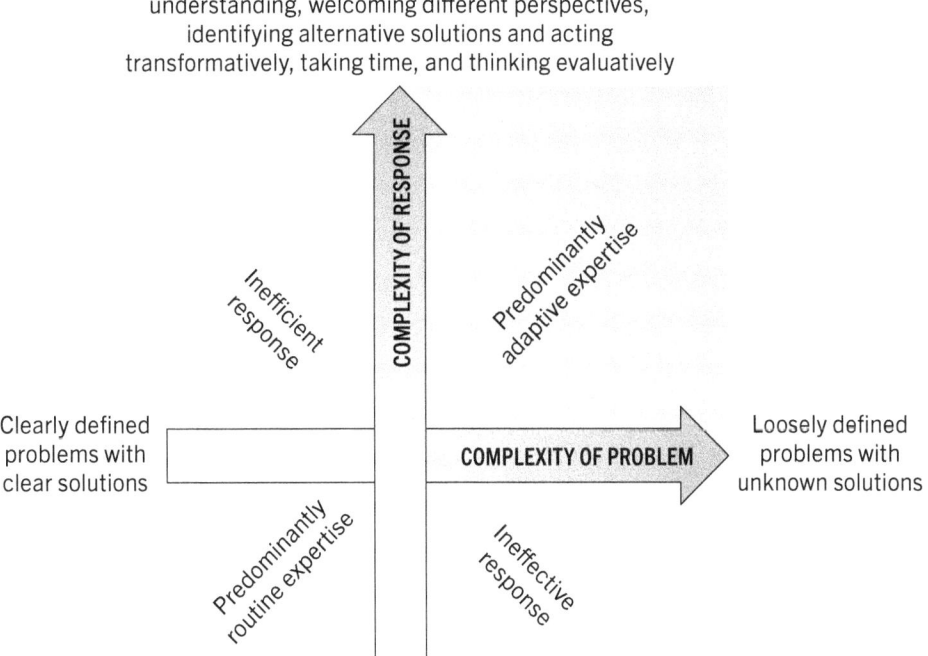

FIGURE 1.3 Matching expertise to the complexity of problems

Source: Le Fevre D, Timperley H, Twyford K, Ell F (2020) *Leading powerful professional learning: responding to complexity with adaptive expertise*, Corwin and Learning Forward, Thousand Oaks, California. Used with permission.

Figure 1.3 (see p. 7) identifies the importance of matching the complexity of the problem to the kind of learning and expertise required to address it. When problems are clearly defined with clear solutions, they are best addressed through developing routine expertise. It is efficient. If a beginning teacher, for example, has little idea of how to set up the basics of a learning environment, then this is best taught directly though modelling and description. However, when the problem is loosely defined, the causes unclear, with multiple possible solutions, then is it important to develop adaptive expertise through the conversations described in this book. Complicated challenges often become complex – they form a continuum, rather than a dichotomy, as one merges into another. For example, once the beginning teacher has the basics of classroom organisation mastered, it is important to inquire into which students feel they belong as a result of the way things are organised, which students feel alienated, what kind of learning is promoted through the classroom set up, whose culture does it reflect, and what is the impact on students' motivation. A whole new set up may be required because routines, even as basic as classroom organisation, can have unexpected consequences.

Attributes of adaptive expertise

The conversations illustrated in this book are about developing adaptive expertise. They are about addressing the complexity inherent in most educational challenges. It may be a situation where some area of achievement is low, some students are demonstrating anxiety or a new principal is developing a strategic plan. Before describing the conversations, however, it is important to be more specific about what constitutes adaptive expertise.

The touchstone for all thinking and actions in adaptive expertise is to make more of a difference to students' learning and wellbeing. Given that equity issues are so prominent in our education systems, this needs to be a focus. Adaptive expertise is also driven by curiosity about what is happening for learners and those who have responsibility for teaching them, and if the solutions to particular challenges are making a difference. In this way, inquiry is also central to adaptive expertise.

My colleagues and I have identified 6 core attributes, or ways of thinking, acting and inquiring, that further unpack the idea of adaptive expertise. These include thinking and acting evaluatively, knowledgeably, metacognitively, collaboratively, responsively and systemically, with inquiry underpinning them all.

Figure 1.4 illustrates how these attributes of inquiring, thinking and acting that underpin adaptive expertise work together to drive the decisions and actions necessary to make a difference to student learning and wellbeing. They are shown as an ongoing loop to emphasise their interdependent, holistic nature and their inherent fluidity as educators adapt and respond to complex challenges. Student, learning and wellbeing are encircled by the attributes, highlighting the centrality of these outcomes to adaptive expertise.

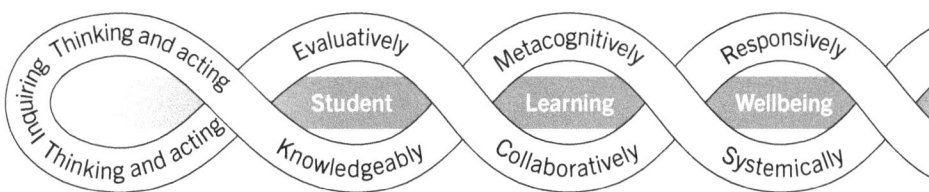

FIGURE 1.4 Attributes of adaptive expertise in educational leadership

Source: Timperley H, Twyford K (2021) 'Adaptive expertise in educational leadership: embracing complexity in leading today's schools', *Australian Educational Leadership*, 44(1):8–12. Adapted and used with permission.

Table 1.1 elaborates each of the 6 attributes identified in Figure 1.4 and contrasts how they are sometimes interpreted from a routine expertise perspective.

TABLE 1.1 Contrasting adaptive and routine expertise in relation to 6 key attributes

Attributes of adaptive expertise	How they might be interpreted from a routine expertise perspective
1. Thinking and acting evaluatively about impact on student outcomes	
Thinking evaluatively about your and others' impact means constantly inquiring into the ways in which organisational, leadership, teaching and community practices come together to influence the learning and wellbeing of all students, then acting on that information.	Thinking evaluatively about impact usually involves collecting evidence of student learning but rarely leads to an analysis of the complexity of multiple influences that impact student learning.

continued →

Attributes of adaptive expertise	How they might be interpreted from a routine expertise perspective
2. Seeking deep knowledge to make more of a difference	
Thinking about what you need to know and do to increase your impact leads to actively seeking and using that knowledge to make more of a difference to all students.	New knowledge is acquired incrementally, without the participating professionals necessarily believing it is essential or useful to make a difference to student learning and wellbeing.
3. Thinking metacognitively	
Thinking metacognitively about your actions and decision-making must result in surfacing and challenging your own and others' theories and inquiring into your beliefs and biases, so you can identify what needs to change to make more of a difference.	The focus of improvement is on practice, rather than on the beliefs underpinning those practices, or on challenging potential biases known to impact equity in relation to student learning and wellbeing.
4. Working collaboratively	
Working collaboratively requires building relational trust and collective efficacy to make more of a difference to student learning and wellbeing. Working collaboratively involves inquiring into others' beliefs and knowledge and is likely to lead to innovative solutions.	Working collaboratively is often more focused on the educators (e.g. their relationships and participation) rather than the impact of the collaboration on student outcomes.
5. Thinking and acting responsively	
Thinking and acting responsively is about bringing together the information generated through the previous 4 attributes to make a difference to the needs of all learners. It means seeking the unknown, the uncertain and the unexpected, responding to them in new ways and persisting until learner outcomes for all have improved.	What is already known is used to best meet the needs of learners without necessarily seeking new information, persisting until learner outcomes have improved or rethinking approaches when they have not.

Attributes of adaptive expertise	How they might be interpreted from a routine expertise perspective
6. Thinking and acting systemically	
Thinking systemically means recognising complexity and developing coherence among improvement activities to increase their impact and sustainability. It requires a dual focus of inquiring into the 'big picture' for improvement, while ensuring the direction of travel on the ground is having the desired impact on student outcomes.	Improvement is undertaken as 'bits' and 'bites' (e.g. a new pedagogical practice, better understanding of an aspect of the curriculum, or shared leadership) without a bigger picture analysis or ensuring that all the activity is leading to the desired impact on student outcomes.

Source: Timperley H, Twyford K (2021) 'Adaptive expertise in educational leadership: embracing complexity in leading today's schools', *Australian Educational Leadership*, 44(1):8–12. Used with permission.

These attributes are underpinned by a set of educational and interpersonal values. At their core, they are about promoting deep transferrable learning (Pellegrino and Hilton 2012) in ways that develop interpersonal trust and respect (Bryk and Schneider 2002; Goddard et al. 2009; Tschannen-Moran 2001). This means genuinely valuing deep conceptual knowledge and wanting to use that knowledge responsively to promote the learning of all students together with those responsible for educating them. It means reflecting metacognitively about the impact on others and whether the intention is manipulation or a mutual desire to learn.

All these attributes are underpinned by the value of unrelenting curiosity (Timperley et al. 2014); curiosity about what is going on for learners and those responsible for teaching them, curiosity about the latest research that might inform practice, curiosity about a student's cultural heritage to ensure some groups of students are not alienated from school, and curiosity about how your thinking and actions are affecting others.

Over time, these values, together with the associated attributes of adaptive expertise, build school-wide cultures focused on student learning and wellbeing. Conversations become much easier as all parties share an understanding that this is their purpose. As educators' confidence builds in using conversations to address complex challenges and develop adaptive expertise, their focus shifts more strongly towards genuine inquiry. The participants become comfortable with uncertainty and tolerate the ambiguity of not knowing as they navigate the complex challenges to make more of a difference.

Conversations to develop adaptive expertise

Conversations to develop adaptive expertise are fundamentally different from those designed to develop routine expertise. In a review of professional conversations with impact (Timperley 2015), I identified 5 enablers that come together in these types of conversations. As with complex challenges, none of these enablers can be addressed without including the others, because the parts come together in many different ways to form a whole. The enablers are identified in Figure 1.5 and elaborated in the sections that follow.

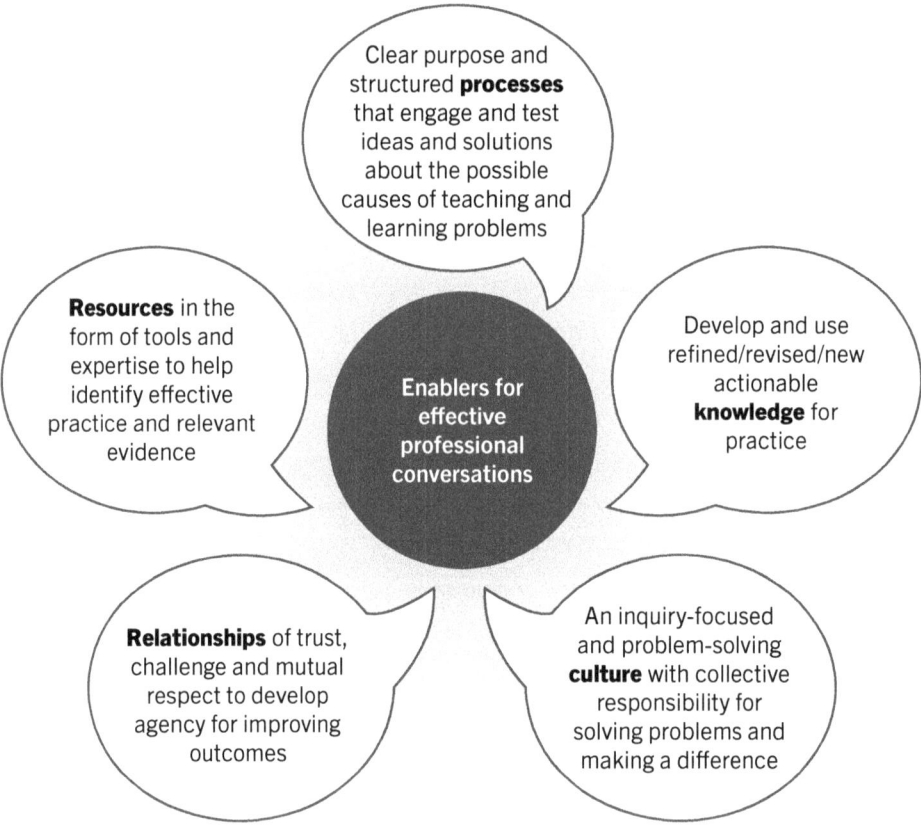

FIGURE 1.5 Enablers for effective conversations

Source: Timperley H (2015) *Professional conversations and improvement-focused feedback*, AITSL, Melbourne. Used with permission.

1. Relationships

Relationships of trust and mutual respect are fundamental to conversations if they are to promote professional learning. These relationships are developed through having the conversations and do not need to exist prior. This means that every conversation needs to be respectful of the participants and promote trust.

Much has been written about relational trust and its importance in contributing to improved outcomes for students (for example, Bryk and Schneider 2002). In essence, relational trust can be summed up as relationships where there is 'a willingness to accept risk on the basis of judgements that a trusted party is benevolent, honest, reliable, and competent' (Goddard et al. 2009:296).

However, I want to highlight some additional aspects that came through a conversational analysis I undertook for the Australian Institute for Teaching and School Leadership (AITSL) (Timperley 2015). Relationships encompassing trust need also to include challenge, accompanied by high expectations that things will change and improve. Without the challenge and high expectations, those participating in the conversation may feel supported, but there is little evidence that improvement will result. On the other hand, Twyford et al. (2017) found that when there is too much challenge, learning is limited and not much changes, except increased anxiety and feelings of vulnerability.

Challenge needs to result in the educators participating in the conversations believing they can make a difference and being committed to doing so. This is summarised in the phrase 'developing professional agency'. Agency can be undermined by a lack of clarity, a lack of skills or knowledge or a lack of motivation. Effective conversations unpack both the potential for agency and elements that may inhibit it and seek to address these.

Listening for the following type of statement can help to reveal if the conversations are developing agency:

> I now know why that didn't work and what I need to do differently.

2. Resources to support professional learning

Tools (or, more aptly, 'artefacts') and expertise both shape conversations and influence their success. Artefacts give powerful messages about what is important and careful consideration needs to be given to these messages. Given the centrality of student learning to adaptive expertise, a common artefact is evidence of student learning. But it is more complex than this and attention needs to be given to the form of the artefact. For example, if this evidence is in the form of state or national benchmarks, with no other information, the messages likely to be conveyed include:

- Student achievement at a given standard matters.
- Achievement is more important than progress.
- Diagnosis is not needed for progress to be accelerated – the information is in the grades themselves.
- Any problems identified reside in the students' abilities or attitudes.

On the other hand, the messages are very different if the evidence is in the form of the written work of struggling students, assessed using descriptive criteria, together with a video of the teacher working with the students and student input.

Artefacts may also be in the form of protocols, diagrams or developmental continua – all of which are intended to convey important messages. Inquiring into how the users of a resource are interpreting the key messages can help to inform and shape conversations. Two potentially powerful questions include:

Tell me what key ideas this resource (evidence, artefact) conveys to you?
Do you find the resource useful [in this situation]?

Professional expertise is the second kind of resource needed to promote learning through conversations. The role of this expertise is to focus and shape new professional learning and the development of professional practices to address complex challenges. Leaders often need to have, or to be able to draw on, different kinds of expertise. For example, a principal may be facing a challenge to shift teaching practice from a 'transmission and production' approach to one more compatible with 'learning for life'. The principal will need expertise in both teaching and in leading change. An important question here is:

Who has the expertise to help unpack and address this particular challenge?

Another form of expertise is in the conversations themselves. In the example of the principal who is trying to shift teaching practice it may be important to work out why previous attempts to shift teaching practice have failed. The additional question becomes:

Who has the skills to lead a conversation with leaders and teachers that unpacks what has happened in the past so those involved can decide together what needs to happen next?

3. Clear purpose and structured processes

Clarity of purpose and process contribute to developing trust (Lencioni 2002) and help to reduce feelings of uncertainty and vulnerability (Twyford et al. 2017). A lack of clarity can lead to confusion and a lack of commitment. For this reason, the purpose and process of any professional conversation needs to be clear and agreed at the outset. Those leading conversations often assume others have a shared understanding of the purpose and process, when this is not the case. One way to check is to include a statement and inquiry near the beginning of any conversation, such as:

> My understanding is that we are meeting today to … Is that your understanding or is there something else you want to talk about?

Those leading conversations are typically balancing the need for a structured, predictable purpose and process, while being sufficiently flexible to allow those involved to express, engage and test different ideas. This balancing act requires leaders to collaboratively develop a shared purpose and process, rather than asking lots of questions or telling the other person what to think. It involves engaging ideas about possibilities and negotiating the way forward together.

4. Actionable professional knowledge

Developing professional knowledge, skills and dispositions is the main purpose for having these conversations. In order to have an impact on practice, those involved need to know how to put new knowledge into action. Knowledge without action has no impact. It is here that the differences between routine and adaptive expertise come into play. The development of routine expertise usually helps a leader or teacher to implement a particular practice in a given context. An example may be following a series of steps or a specific program. Such expertise may solve an immediate problem. Adaptive expertise requires the new knowledge to be understood at a sufficiently deep theoretical level that those involved understand the implications across a range of contexts. As Pellegrino and Hilton (2012) describe, deep knowledge is transferable knowledge. Questions that prompt deep knowledge include:

> Why did/didn't this work?

New actionable knowledge usually arises from a mix of formal knowledge established through research and leaders' or colleagues' knowledge, together with an individual's existing personal knowledge. All these forms of knowledge need to be engaged and deepened to promote professional learning in ways that make a difference.

5. An inquiry-focused culture

Cultures are integral to all organisations whether they are state departments, regional offices or schools. One way to decide if these cultures are learning cultures is to listen to whether the conversations are focused on what others should be doing, or if they are focused on the contribution of the key actors themselves. The first kind of culture can be summarised as 'everyone but me' or 'If only they would …'. The second includes conversations that sound more like 'everyone including me'. Questions revealing an inquiry culture include:

> I wonder what is happening here?
> What do we need to do together to make the difference?

To make a difference to student learning, ultimately challenges must be addressed. But many educational conversations jump to solutions too soon and are dominated by 'solutionitis', a term coined by Bryk and Schneider (2002). This occurs when immediate solutions are suggested to complex challenges – the new program, the additional middle leadership position, the professional development course – without exploring the following questions:

> What is the real problem here?
> What are the possible multiple causes that are contributing to it?

An inquiry culture uses evidence to add to the pool of information rather than to prove a point. All evidence requires interpretation to be useful and the same evidence is likely to be interpreted in different ways by different participants in a conversation. Saving all the evidence to 'prove your point' is likely to be met with defensiveness. Bringing evidence to discuss, interpret and to shed light on some possibilities is more likely to promote professional learning.

Outline of the book

The following 4 chapters of this book are designed to offer a progression of depth and challenge in professional conversations. Chapter 2 is an introduction to the specifics of professional conversations and is titled 'Getting started'. It includes the role of evidence, building actionable knowledge and genuine inquiry. Chapter 3 is about 'Going deeper' and includes strategies such as building theoretical knowledge, unpacking theories of practice, and acknowledging emotion and vulnerability. Chapter 4 is at a more expert level and brings in more challenging constructs, such as developing metacognition and revealing unconscious bias. Chapter 4 also includes some examples of how to work in teams in ways that are consistent with the values and strategies highlighted throughout the book. Chapter 5 specifically focuses on formal observations of practice and improvement-oriented feedback. How the material in these different parts evolve is outlined in Figure 1.6.

FIGURE 1.6 An overview of the focus of the different chapters

Although these chapters are sequenced at increasing levels of complexity, it does not mean starting at the beginning and ending at the end. The framing in terms of adaptive expertise means starting where it is most meaningful for you to do so, backtracking if necessary, or fast forwarding if it enhances your professional learning. Those with adaptive expertise take responsibility for seeking feedback, identifying their own professional learning needs and engaging with relevant knowledge and skills to meet those needs.

Each of the strategies in the different chapters are illustrated with conversations. For reasons of clarity, they are typically between 2 people. However, all the strategies can be applied to both large and small groups because the learning theory underpinning them holds for all these situations (Dumont et al. 2010; Bransford et al. 2000; Pellegrino and Hilton 2012). A specific example of working with a group is provided at the end of Chapter 4.

All the conversations used to illustrate the different strategies in each chapter are based on real conversations provided by a variety of educators, including those located in schools, district, regional and state offices in Australia. Their task in these conversations was to promote the professional learning of leaders and teachers and to develop their adaptive expertise. I collected and analysed the conversation transcripts during the course of my work across multiple educational jurisdictions. I have edited and altered most of the conversations, have used pseudonyms and have identified the participants using generic position descriptors for obvious reasons. For readers based in schools, I have provided context by using position descriptors including school principal (SP), associate principal (AP), deputy principal (DP), senior leader (SL), team leader (TL), professional learning community leader (PLCL), faculty leader (FL), leader (L) and teacher (T). For those based in state-level positions, I have used the generic term of regional leader (RL). Most of the transcripts also contain my own notes highlighting particular strategies used; these are included as italics in square brackets.

Different jurisdictions and schools refer to groups of teachers meeting for the purpose of improving practice in a number of different ways. I have used generic designations for groups who have formalised approaches, including professional learning communities (PLCs), inquiry teams and faculty teams. At other times, I have referred to them as team meetings.

No one improves their professional conversations by reading about them alone. This book is unlikely to help you, unless you are prepared, through a formative assessment process, to record and analyse your conversations with others who are developing expertise in professional learning conversations (James and Pollard

2011; Wiliam 2011). This recording becomes the evidence of your practice for you to work with. Around 10 to 15 minutes is usually enough. As with any formative assessment process, the analysis needs to be undertaken in relation to criteria for effective conversations, otherwise it is likely to be superficial (for example, 'I talked too much' or 'I'll never say "um" again'). These criteria are not relevant to the challenge of promoting professional learning and developing adaptive expertise. The criteria that are relevant are developed with increasing complexity through each chapter.

Along with other material, the criteria for effective conversations template and a planning framework template are provided as supplementary digital resources designed to accompany the chapters in this book. Details of how to access the digital resources can be found on page 116. It is important to experiment, celebrate success, possibly get frustrated with your own expectations and try again.

Engagement in these activities is much more likely to promote your professional learning if you undertake them with someone who has specific expertise in professional conversations. It is just too hard to be objective in something as personal as having conversations. Working with colleagues you respect and trust is fundamental to professional learning that involves risk-taking, experimentation, potential confrontation of treasured beliefs and development of new patterns of action.

CHAPTER 2
Getting started

Introduction

This second chapter outlines some basics of conversations designed to deepen professional learning and increase impact. The strategies form the beginnings of developing adaptive expertise. Each section in this chapter begins by describing the key features of the strategy and illustrates each one with examples of conversations. Some of the examples are between school leaders and teachers. Others are between regional leaders and school leaders. Each section also has 'thinking prompts' to consider because thinking underpins what is said. The strategies described in this chapter are summarised in Figure 2.1.

FIGURE 2.1 Features of conversations described in Chapter 2: Getting started

At the end of the chapter, a planning process for professional conversations is outlined, together with a task and criteria to analyse a conversation using the features described in this chapter.

Establish the purpose and focus

This first strategy may appear to be self-evident as the starting point of all professional conversations but the evidence from my analysis of many conversations is it is often skipped over or stated in very general terms. The issue that arises in these situations is that the person initiating the conversation, usually a leader, assumes the other person knows the purpose, and agrees with it. This results in the leader failing to clarify these important foundations prior to getting started. Beginning a conversation without establishing the purpose often leads to confusion, with the other person wondering why they are having the conversation and sometimes looking for the 'hidden agenda' even when there may not be one. Hidden agendas are inconsistent with the values outlined in the introduction and the development of adaptive expertise. A key rule for all these conversations is that there are no surprises. Unpleasant surprises destroy trust.

Establishing the purpose and focus is a balancing act. While clarity establishes trust that there are no 'hidden agendas', it can also be controlling if the person initiating the conversation fails to show sufficient flexibility to accommodate the other person's preferences and priorities. It is important, therefore, to be invitational of the other person's ideas, so they have an opportunity to contribute to the purpose and express issues that are important to them.

💡 THINKING PROMPTS

- What is my purpose and focus for this conversation?
- Why this purpose and focus and not something else?
- Have I considered the other person's preferred purpose and focus? Have I asked?
- How can I state my purpose clearly but in a way that is invitational of the other person's contribution?
- Have we previously agreed on the purpose and is this conversation a continuation of the same agenda? If so, do I need to check?

Compare the different openings to the conversations below. This first is from a regional leader (RL) to a school principal and is controlling with a hidden agenda despite the informal language.

> RL: 'Hi, I wanted to chat with you today about the students who are giving you a hard time' [when you want to talk about the teacher's classroom management because of a number of complaints].

This next one from a school principal (SP) to a teacher is vague and fails to be open about what you want to talk about and why.

> SP: 'Hi, how are things going?' or 'What do you think about …?'

Conversations starting in this way are typically unfocused up to the point when the leader initiating the conversation finally finds an opening for what they want to talk about – which then often comes as a surprise to the other person.

The following examples are both clear and invite the other person to raise issues that are important to them.

In this first example, a senior school leader (SL) has responsibility for focusing faculty meetings on school development priorities. The senior school leader attended a faculty meeting at the invitation of a leader because a teacher was reportedly blocking discussions. The senior school leader opened the follow-up conversation in the following way:

SL: OK, so I wanted to touch base with you following up from being at your faculty meeting the other day and talk about how we can move the faculty forward. Would it still be helpful if we work that out together?

In this second example from a large secondary school, a school principal (SP) wanted to review a difficult reorganisation of the Arts PLC with the PLC leader (PLCL).

SP: I wanted to thank you initially for the support that you've provided to the combined junior and senior PLCs in the arts. I imagine that decision has created some difficulties, some challenges for the group coming together like this and I just thought this might be a good opportunity to talk about some of those challenges and see what we can come up with together in terms of addressing them.

PLCL: Sounds good. There certainly have been challenges.

Negotiating the purpose and focus by a phone call or email in advance can save time, particularly when those having the conversation are not in the same school. The following example of a phone call consists of the opening lines from a regional leader (RL) and a school's team leader (TL).

RL: Thanks for your email and an update on how the testing went on Tuesday. I'm thinking that for tomorrow, focusing on both reading and writing might be too much, so I suggest we focus on the reading part of your email and look at writing another time. Is that ok?

TL: Well, I'd really rather look at inferential comprehension today because it's this term's focus.

These more transparent and inclusive conversations share some key features.

- The purpose is clear with context and reason provided (remember a key rule – no surprises).
- The purpose is checked with the other person in a way they are invited to contribute.

Evidence and artefacts

The role of evidence and artefacts to shape conversations should not be underestimated (Timperley 2015). They are both resources that help to keep the conversations focused. I will begin this section by describing conversations using evidence, with a second part describing the complementary role of other artefacts.

Use evidence to promote professional learning

In the introductory chapter, I drew attention to the idea that evidence contributes to conversations as a source of information. Sometimes people make a distinction between data and evidence, with data being numerical and evidence being more qualitative. I have used the more generic term of evidence to include both numerical and qualitative evidence. Here, evidence refers to an available body of observable phenomena and may comprise numerical data, such as test results; someone's actions, such as teacher/student interactions; or the physical attributes of a situation, such as how students are seated. This definition of evidence differentiates it from its interpretation, which is about making inferences about the meaning of that evidence, such as whether or not the students are making good progress, if the teacher/student interactions are promoting learning or if the seating arrangements allow too much noise.

Referring to evidence in professional conversations develops evaluative thinking, which is fundamental to adaptive expertise. Earl and I (2016) describe evaluative thinking as a systematic way of using evidence to assess progress (or lack of it) in relation to any change or innovation, rather than relying on anecdotes or impressions.

The most important criterion to consider in relation to a specific conversation is the form of evidence that is most useful to promote learning about a given situation. It might be what someone did, what they said, what they wrote, or an artefact they have produced. It is tangible, it can be observed and described.

> **THINKING PROMPTS**
> - What evidence will help to inform the situation and promote professional learning about it?
> - Have I asked the person with whom I am having the conversation about what evidence they think would be useful?

The most useful evidence depends on the context of the conversation. If it is a conversation with a teacher about their teaching, then it is important to have evidence of what and how students are learning, together with the teaching interactions and strategies that are designed to promote that learning.

Evidence about students may be informal; for example, their responses (or lack of response) to a question or request. Or it may be more formal, such as the pattern of answers on an in-class assessment. More systematically collected evidence may include attitudinal survey responses, National Assessment Program Literacy and Numeracy (NAPLAN) results or other test results. Each of these forms of evidence are relevant in different situations. For example, an individual student's non-verbal response is unlikely to be appropriate for cohort assessment of students' wellbeing. However, it might be highly relevant in an assessment of this same individual student's feelings of anxiety and vulnerability.

Evidence about teaching can range from stated beliefs about teaching and learning, interactions within a team meeting or the processes used to examine evidence of student learning. In this professional learning context, the most important attribute is its relevance to the learning and practice that is the focus of the conversation. The purpose for having this evidence is to link the professional practices to the impact of those practices. Self-reports about either professional practices that describe an individual's actions, or the outcomes, in the absence of evidence, are unreliable.

Compare these 2 conversations about students struggling with mental strategies in numeracy. The team leader (TL) is talking to a teacher (T) with a focus on numeracy. The first conversation is evidence-free with the teacher unable to diagnose what is happening, apart from the 'students not getting it'.

T: We're up to addition and subtraction with a range of numbers. They don't seem to be able to get it. They can do it with single digit numbers, but it all falls apart with 2-digit numbers. We've gone over and over it.

TL: Can you tell me a bit more about what is happening, so I have a better picture?

T: Well, as I said, if I give them single digit numbers, they can do it. But as soon as I increase it to 2-digit numbers, no matter how many times we go over it, they can't do it.

This second conversation followed a 10-minute observation by the team leader. In this transcript, and subsequent examples, the italics in square brackets are my analysis; these notes draw attention to particular conversational strategies to highlight the points being illustrated.

TL: I noticed that some of the students didn't have any mental strategies to work with or instant recall. They had to use their fingers or get the counters out to do it, but they knew the concept of subtraction. So, they knew that they were counting back, or they were counting on if they were adding. There were single digit numbers and that led me to think that it was more about mental strategies and fluency, rather than being able to work with a whole range of numbers. Without this fluency, working with 2-digit numbers is likely to be difficult. What do you think?
[Articulates a more sophisticated analysis as a result of the observation]

T: Maybe we went too high, too fast.
[The description of the details helps the teacher to identify the problem they are struggling to articulate.]

TL: Yes, it seems it was pitched a bit too high before fluency in the basics was in place. Let's unpack this a bit more and figure out what was going on and what it means for teaching this and other numeracy concepts.
[The analysis leads to a shared understanding of the problem and the basis for a solution.]

The forms of evidence in conversations about leadership typically relate to the leadership actions and the impact on the thinking and actions of those for whom the leader has responsibility. These people may be teachers or other leaders. For example, in a conversation between a regional leader and a school leader about their leadership of meetings, it is much more grounded if the regional leader has been a direct participant in a meeting led by the school leader. The regional leader is able to observe the interactions between the leader and members of the team and can assess the leader's impact on the team's development. Ideally, there will also be an impact on the outcomes for students, but this may not be relevant in every conversation.

I have put the qualifier 'ideally' in the preceding paragraph because having this evidence is not always practical, particularly early in a relationship, and may not be appropriate for every conversation. The evidence is most important when things are not progressing and the purpose of the conversation is to investigate a way forward. We expect teachers to observe students and their work in order to teach them well. Increasingly, we expect teachers to be observed and have others work alongside them in order to promote their professional learning and improvements to their practice. This linking allows for more targeted professional learning. In the same way, developing leaders is much more effective in improving practice if there is some evidence of their practice (for example, being part of a meeting, an observation, a video or audio recording).

Initially, mistrust may arise if using evidence for professional learning is not a routine part of practice. Trust and respect are built when the purpose for the conversation is negotiated in advance with no hidden agendas, as well as asking others what evidence they would find useful. The more openness in these processes, the less controlling they become, thus creating trust. Evidence of professional practice brings a lens to conversations that promotes learning more rapidly than without it. An example of the significance of using evidence about leadership from my own work is presented in Box 1.1.

Box 1.1. An illustration of the importance of using evidence about leadership

I worked with a group of regional leaders whose key responsibility was to promote an inquiry process with groups of teachers across different schools. The initial sources of evidence I looked at were early and late inquiries (evidence of the outcomes of the regional leaders' work). We agreed that the inquiries were not deepening

continued →

as expected. The leaders described the difficulties they had in helping teachers deepen their inquiries and asked for my help. However, their descriptions did not pinpoint the issues. Before my next visit, I asked them to video their conversation with an inquiry group. It was readily apparent after 5 minutes of video that these regional leaders had assumed a 'reporting' role rather than a 'co-inquiry' role. They asked the teachers to report on what they were doing in their inquiries, and gave suggestions based on these reports, rather than co-working with the teachers on their inquiries, modelling and probing for depth. When I asked why they went about their work in this way, the issue soon became apparent that they, as regional leaders, did not know how to take on this co-working role. This focus became my work with them.

In this next example, a team leader (TL) and senior school leader (SL) were reviewing PLC processes in a secondary school accompanied by evidence in the form of a survey of student attitudes to science. The team leader connected the evidence of changed student attitudes to the teachers planning as a team.

TL: We've been working on developing a shared pedagogy in science. There is much more agreement in the team now than at the beginning of the year.

SL: So, are you seeing, I suppose, good data from your students that the shared pedagogy is having some impact as well?
    [*Draws attention to evidence of outcomes*]

TL: We are, yes. So, the big focus is around the student engagement in science and the willingness to be challenged. And we've done some work around reflecting on the proficiencies, and also attitudes. So, we've done some self-efficacy surveys with kids and brought that to compare. Unfortunately, in hindsight we didn't do a pre-assessment with these kids to compare. But we did last year and so it appears to be a fairly big improvement on that. So, across the cohort, the kids like science better and choose to be challenged and in fact anecdotally my class often complain when they're not.

SL: Fantastic. Have you got the data?
    [*Asks for evidence to check the team leader's interpretation*]

TL: Yes, here.

SL: [Looks at the comparison with the previous year] This is great. So, you see that as a direct result of, I suppose that collective efficacy of your team coming together with that particular pedagogy, and the difference for students. And that's your evidence that the teachers are actually making the changes they're saying they're doing. Because, actually you are seeing the different language coming from the kids, as well as from the teachers.
> [*Articulates their interpretation of the evidence linking student responses to teaching*]

TL: Yes, and I guess with that evidence there's been – there's been a shared planning approach. Before, the difficulty was it was just one person taking responsibility and doing it alone, then telling the others.

SL: Yes.

TL: But the really neat thing now is that the teams actually challenged it and said, 'We've noticed you know, this week that the tasks weren't challenging, or they're not open'.

SL: So now, less of a 'I'll plan it and just flick you whatever you need' versus 'I'll come with an idea and we'll discuss it and flesh it out?'

TL: And it hasn't had to come from me – it has at times come from me – but it's come even from the likes of Susie who initially was someone who …

SL: … who wasn't sure it was going to work for her.
> [*Draws attention to how the evidence has influenced efficacy (linking teaching and learning)*]

TL: What's changed for her is how the kids are talking and their attitudes to science. So, she's convinced.

Use artefacts and expertise to promote professional learning

Effective teachers prepare resources for the students. In the same way, leaders and mentors should prepare resources to promote professional learning in the area of focus because these resources shape what is learned and how it is learned. Depending on the context, these resources are likely to relate to leadership, change management, curriculum, pedagogy and assessment. One regional leader described how they needed to have 'deep pockets' from which they drew appropriate resources depending on how conversations with principals progressed and the issues that arose. In reality, the 'deep pockets' took the form of a basket in which resources were collected in anticipation of challenges likely to arise each day.

Leaders should also consider if the right expertise will be in the room or accessible to participants. As educational processes become more sophisticated, so does the expertise required. Depending on the type of learning being promoted, expertise can include knowledge of curriculum, pedagogical practices, change management, regulations, human resources, digital technologies, data analysis and evaluation. No one person can know everything, but it does require a level of confidence to be vulnerable about one's own expertise and to be able to say:

> 'Let me get back to you about that when I have consulted …' or 'I think it would be helpful if Roger came to our next meeting because this is his area of expertise'.

Engage beliefs

In any learning situation, whether student or professional, it is important to inquire into the learners' beliefs that underpin their current practice. Everyone does things for a reason, and unless those reasons are unearthed in ways that allow them to be examined and that show why they might get in the way (or not), the practices are unlikely to change in any substantive sense. These reasons and the associated practice are usually referred to as personal theories. The first principle in the well-known research on how people learn, as articulated by Bransford et al. (2000), is the importance of engaging learners' theories about how the world works.

Personal theories are, by definition, personal, and form part of a professional's identity. It is here that mutual respect and inquiry are paramount. Often this involves taking a step back, giving time and space for exploration of these theories and the beliefs on which they are based, rather than rushing to challenge.

Learning, however, depends on engagement with alternative theories. So, it is equally important that the leader of the conversation brings these alternatives to the table. Again, a stance of appreciation and inquiry demonstrates personal respect. This is where expertise comes into both the leader's conversational skills and knowledge of the research underpinning particular practices. Leaders need to be conversant with the theory and research that is likely to apply to a particular situation, including why it is likely to be effective and how it can be enacted in the educator's context. This is fundamental to adaptive expertise.

Personal theories are not static. Rather, these theories change and adapt in response to new information. If professional learning is to lead to improved practice, those involved in conversations where personal theories are in competition with one another, each participant needs to express their theories, reveal the reasoning underpinning them and inquire into the other person's theory. Ideally, they will need to resolve the differences if they are able to. How to do this effectively is elaborated in Chapter 3.

💡 THINKING PROMPTS
- Do I know what the other person believes and is thinking or am I assuming this?
- Have I expressed my beliefs clearly and in ways that invite the other person to engage with them or challenge them?

In this next transcript, a senior leader (SL) both engages a team leader's (TL) personal theories and articulates an alternative around the use of an inquiry approach in mathematics. The senior leader, new to the school, had found shifting the Kindergarten to Year 2 team from whole class 'chalk and talk' very challenging. The senior leader decided to work initially with the junior school team leader to plan and co-teach an inquiry approach to mathematics before working with the whole team. At this point in the conversation, the team leader agreed that the inquiry approach had led to higher levels of student engagement and learning.

SL: So where to next with this planning of inquiry approaches in the classroom? I know it's something that I have been advocating because of the way it promotes mathematical thinking. I'm not sure you or the team have been convinced. So, we had planned to present the ideas from this lesson to the rest of your team. From what we've done in the planning and co-teaching and the student work samples that we've evaluated, what do you think? Is this something that could be a regular occurrence in your classroom?
[*Expresses reasons for advocating an inquiry approach; probes for personal theories that may be in competition*]

TL: It could definitely be a regular occurrence within the classroom. I think that the students really enjoyed having that open-ended experience where they were able to come up with all the different combinations and work collaboratively together. The questions can change but the skills and the problem-solving and the critical thinking can be applied in any context really with any question that's given to them so it's definitely something that they enjoy doing. And I think in that way the students got a lot out of it.

> [*Most conversations stop at the end of this statement by the team leader and fail to probe why the team had not taken up an inquiry approach earlier. This next part of the conversation was essential for resolving theories in competition.*]

SL: Mmmm ... I'm curious as to as to why an inquiry approach hasn't been an option before. It's not a new idea by any means, but it hasn't been taken up by any of the team.

> [*Once again, probes for theories in competition with an inquiry approach*]

TL: I think that's because I was so set on doing whole class lessons or say guided maths groups where you're working with different ability groups. Yes, so I guess with this, it's more whole class, right, and I guess the tasks like this do have access for all the students. But some of the students may need that explicit teaching of actual strategies. So, teaching them how to actually add, and how to subtract or doing simple strategies to get to that, I feel like the inquiry approach sometimes will transfer that knowledge, but they need to know those strategies to be able to apply them.

> [*Reveals her thinking, which is likely to be in competition with the senior leader's theory*]

SL: Right. So, can you see how to include that explicit teaching in the inquiry approach? How I was thinking about it was we use the engine room for explicit teaching during numeracy groups. Does that seem like a possibility to include it then?

> [*Looks to resolve the competition between the 2 theories*]

TL: I think that we would still need some of that explicit teaching within the classroom and this could be once a week, or once a fortnight, or something like that so it could be like a problem-solving session where they're still learning those explicit strategies, but they're having an opportunity to have that transfer and to apply those strategies in a different context so it's not just numeracy.

> *[Team leader demonstrates understanding of how to integrate their own personal theory and the new way of teaching]*

SL: Thanks for bringing that up. Yes, I think what would work is what you have said about explicit teaching while inquiry is happening, as well as in the engine room time as it relates to number, so there would be that connection. Transfer from one situation to another is important.

TL: I'm just visualising how this will all look. I do think this is achievable. I guess I can use inquiry questions in the classroom, you know at least once a week, and then taking those students and explicitly teaching them those strategies. Those ones that aren't getting it and teaching them those strategies. Yes, and I will talk to my team about the success of this in my classroom and how they too can do it their own classrooms. During our meeting this week, would you be able to present this with me to the team?

> *[Demonstrates they are now thinking about how to put the new knowledge into action]*

Build actionable knowledge

All the attributes of the conversations described so far in this book are for the purpose of building actionable knowledge, that is, knowledge that can be used to improve leading, teaching and learning.

In the conversation above about an inquiry approach to mathematics, the senior school leader, attempting to resolve competing personal theories, asks the team leader if they can envisage how to include explicit teaching in an inquiry approach. The senior school leader then offers a suggestion about how this can be done and invites feedback. After some discussion, the team leader responds with the specifics of how they might integrate the numeracy strategies into an inquiry approach. This transcript shows the team leader thinking through how they will put their new knowledge into practice. Developing agency for professional learning and changes in practice in this way is essential in any conversation about improving practice.

There are several ways in which mentors and leaders can build actionable knowledge in conversations. These include:

- introducing new knowledge
- extending knowledge when it becomes apparent the other person's knowledge is limited
- elaborating practical descriptions by linking them to more theoretical ideas, focusing on reasons why a particular practice should be effective
- challenging problematic ideas.

In the following transcript, a team leader (TL) is discussing how to make judgements about junior students' reading levels with an early career teacher (T) in the middle of Term 4. The teacher has entered the level for each student in one column but has left blank a second column headed 'Processing behaviours'. An important starting point is to determine the teacher's current knowledge in order to decide the best strategy to develop it further. During the conversation, the team leader ascertained that this teacher needed to develop new knowledge if they were to enter information into the second column.

TL: Okay, so we agreed earlier to talk about how we're making judgements about reading text levels, both in terms of end-of-year reporting, but also in terms of the way in which we're tracking student growth and looking at student behaviours.
[*Checks previously agreed purpose*]

T: I've got the students' levels here [brings out sheet with text levels recorded].
[*Uses evidence to inform the conversation*]

TL: Ok. That's good and it's really up to date. I was wondering how you decided on the level because you haven't made any comments about their processing in this column.
[*Probes teacher's thinking about the absence of evidence*]

T: I listen to them read and if they can work it out, then I enter the level. I wasn't sure what you wanted me to put in the processing behaviours column.

TL: So, I just want to check – the information you are using is mostly about whether or not they can read the right words?

T: Yes.

TL: That might hide that they are reading it accurately, but they can't talk about the strategies they use or what the text means. So that's what we want in the processing behaviours column. If they don't self-correct, for example, then it causes problems down the track, especially when they're transitioning into Year 2. They think reading is about getting the right words when it is really about understanding the meaning of the text. And if that is what goes home in the end-of-year reporting, then parents think they are doing better than they are. So, getting the words right is only one of the behaviours.

> [*Builds actionable knowledge by challenging and extending the teacher's knowledge of reading*]

T: I talk about self-correcting and sounding out words and they seem to understand.

TL: It's about being really tuned in to each child when talking about the reading strategies they are using. What is going on in their heads? What kind of meaning are they giving to it?

> [*Builds actionable knowledge through extending limited knowledge*]

T: I'm not sure what to record …

TL: I think this is something we could all revisit as a team, so we'll do that next week. Rather than go into it now, I wanted to explore a bit more about why we should worry about processing, because there are a few more behaviours we need to notice. Let's put that to one side for now. I think what I've got from this is that 'processing behaviours' column [indicates the recording sheet] needs to have a lot more detail and I'd like to spend some time thinking about that. So, let's return to the 'why' it is important.

> [*Makes a strategic decision that better resources would support knowledge building; deepens knowledge by focusing on reasons*]

T: So we can report it to parents.

TL: Well, that's kind of on everyone's mind at this time of the year. But the real reason is for planning so you can ensure your teaching is at the point of each student's need.

> [*Builds knowledge for potential action by focusing on reasons*]

T: I feel I haven't really mastered the whole planning thing. I'm confused about how am I supposed to record the levels, planning

and all that. I'm just trying to just, you know, work with the kids. So, I guess that's something I need to figure out.
[*Demonstrates very limited knowledge – a huge learning agenda!*]

💡 THINKING PROMPT
- Have I left the other person with new knowledge aligned to the agreed purpose for the conversation and checked they are able to put it into practice?

Genuine inquiry

While inquiry is the basis for developing adaptive expertise, many inquiries are closer to pseudo-inquiry than to genuine inquiry. Pseudo-inquiry is readily recognised by others and leads to mistrust. The key differences between genuine and pseudo-inquiry are summarised in Table 2.1, with a more theoretical elaboration provided in a paper by Le Fevre et al. (2018).

TABLE 2.1 Comparing genuine and pseudo-inquiry

Genuine inquiry	Pseudo-inquiry
Asking questions you don't know the answer to and genuinely wanting the other person's perspective	Asking questions that you think you probably know the answer to. Either you don't want to say what you think, or you want to know if the other person agrees.
Giving reasons for your questions to make them transparent	Assuming the other person knows the reasons you are asking the question or not stating the reasons because you don't want to disclose them
Gathering evidence to use as the basis for exploring possibilities	Gathering evidence to confirm or prove your point of view
Being aware of your assumptions and open to the idea that you need to check them	Assuming that what you think is correct and needing to 'influence' or 'persuade' others to come to your point of view
Including yourself and your actions as possible contributors to issues in the learning environment – 'everyone including me'	Assuming that if other people change what they are thinking or doing, things would be better – 'everyone but me'

Intention is the best indicator of genuine or pseudo-inquiry, but intentions are difficult to ascertain from a transcript. The thinking behind the question is more important than what is articulated. However, there are conversational forms that are likely to be indicative of which kind of inquiry is being engaged.

One indicator of genuine or pseudo-inquiry is the kinds of questions asked and the frequency with which they are asked. A genuine inquiry question is one for which the person answering the question understands the reasons for it being asked. Including the reason for asking a question ensures that the inquiry is transparent with no hidden agendas. Questions without reasons are often indicative of pseudo-inquiry, where the respondent is essentially being asked to 'guess what's in my head'. After a series of questions, the respondent usually gives the correct answer. If there are more than 2 questions in a sequence (question – answer – question – answer) with no reason given, the process is likely to be pseudo-inquiry. Of course, it is possible to ask pseudo-inquiry questions by giving reasons that are not the real reasons but are rather designed to lead the other person to come up with the 'right' answer.

Some genuine inquiry questions do not have reasons accompanying them, but the problem in the context of professional conversations is they do not reveal to the other person why the leader is asking the question. So, it often feels like pseudo-inquiry from the recipient's point of view.

Compare the following 2 questions. The first is from the earlier transcript about an inquiry approach to teaching mathematics. There is a clear reason for asking the question and it lets the team leader into the senior leader's thinking.

> SL: I'm curious as to as to why an inquiry approach hasn't been an option before. It's not a new idea by any means, but it hasn't been taken up by any of the team.

A more common form of this question, which often elicits a defensive reaction might be:

> SL: Why haven't you used an inquiry approach in the past?

Questions that come at the end of a statement are usually checking questions – for understanding or agreement. Provided they are not leading questions, they are likely to be genuine inquiry. See this example from the transcript in the previous section where the team leader checks with the teacher about reading text levels:

TL: So, I just want to check – the information you are using is mostly about whether or not they can read the right words?

💡 THINKING PROMPT

- Rather than thinking, 'What is my next question?', ask yourself, 'What do I want to know and why do I want to know it?' Then express your thoughts in this way to the other person.

In this next example, a secondary school principal (SP) and team leader (TL) are reviewing the team leader's role with a view to maximising impact. The principal genuinely inquires and gives their reasons because they want to base the review on the experiences and views of the team leader.

SP: Hi Steve, we talked earlier about reviewing your team leader role. It's been new this year and timely for us to have a look and think if there are ways we can organise it for greater impact for next year. So, first let's talk about how it's gone for you this year.
   [*Restates an earlier agreed purpose with a reason*]

TL: So, I guess it's been interesting to come completely out of the classroom. And managing it with other leadership roles – you know it all merges, where the one role ends and the other one begins.

SP: What did you find interesting in terms of completely coming out of the classroom? Can you just clarify that for me, so I understand it better?
   [*A genuine inquiry with a reason*]

TL: I guess for me I felt a little bit – and it was just the way I felt – it was almost like I felt like I'd lose credibility. I don't think anyone ever thought it or said it, or … I wanted to make sure that I still could walk the walk. So, the modelling gave that to me, but what it didn't give was a consistent knowledge of the students I was going into work with. So, I felt like I was going in cold to a lot of the students, and so that you couldn't prepare your questions, or you

SP:	couldn't do the best job of modelling what you were doing because you weren't sure quite where they were specifically. It's difficult, you know, when you're used to keeping your finger on the pulse of your own classes.
SP:	I think I now know what you are saying. I certainly haven't heard any negative comments so you can rest assured on that one. Is there anything else we need to think about for planning your role next year? Keeping in mind it's about having an impact on the teaching and learning.

[*A genuine inquiry with the reason clear from earlier discussion*]

TL: I think it might make more impact if we chunk the time. Because the other thing is sometimes when I go into classes I feel like there's a bit of a show when I go in. You don't want, 'Someone's here to watch'.

SP: And this year we focused your work around the teachers' PDP goal, so I was thinking about reflecting on our whole process. You know we had our whole-school focus, and then we had our learning walks around that whole-school focus and then, I suppose, your work with the teachers was a separate line to that. How do you think that worked for you and for the teachers?

[*A genuine inquiry with a reason stated*]

TL: Most of them had feedback as their goal, which worked well. They were very good at choosing their goals, I must say. And most of them did really well.

SP: So, coming back to the impact, how did you know that they were doing well? How did you monitor the growth of the teacher?

[*A genuine inquiry with the reason clear from earlier parts of the transcript; asks for evidence*]

TL: So, I work out with the teacher a more specific focus than just feedback in general. Which curriculum area and what type of feedback and where they were on the continuum that we've been working with in our team. So, I'd do an observation at that focused time, so this was for Tim, so he wanted a focus on feedback on group discussions. So, that was specific. So, what we did is, I just wrote the feedback he gave, then we went back and had a look at it together and used the continuum for assessing his feedback. We worked out where he was and where he wanted to be, what he needed to do to get there. Had he planned those things? Had he thought about the feedback he might give? So those were the things we did.

[Refers to the continuum as an artefact to promote learning]

SP: This sounds like a great process. And what was the impact?

TL: Everyone made some progress on the continuum. Tim and Selina got to the expert level. The others had lower starting points and progressed at least 2 levels, but they need more support to get to the expert level. What they struggled with is stopping the feedback becoming very glib like, 'Are we going to do the "road signs" sort of feedback?' You know and that's not actually what you want.

SP: So, it's balancing routinised feedback that may not be hitting the mark with really understanding high-quality feedback. I think you are really hitting the mark here. However, I'm wondering about impact on student learning and if this can be a way to help teachers focus on quality and purpose, rather than just 'giving feedback'. Have you focused on that at all?

[Refers to the need for evidence of student learning; asks a checking question with the reason stated before it]

TL: I haven't got to that yet.

SP: So, let's work out a way to do that, connecting the feedback to student learning, and make it a focus for next year. Would that be useful?

[Asks a checking question with the reason implied but clear]

Relationships and co-inquiry

As noted in Chapter 1, relationships of trust, mutual respect and challenge are central to all professional learning. Relationships that heighten vulnerability and stress are more likely to lead to compliance than to learning. On the other hand, relationships that offer support without challenge are unlikely to lead to change and improvement.

The approaches to genuine inquiry that are illustrated above typically take the form of co-inquiry. It is very much about 'working with' rather than 'doing to'. Challenges are unpacked together and meanings probed together, with alternatives taking the form of suggestions that need to be worked through, rather than requirements that are decided in advance. When the purpose is to persuade, rather than to inquire and work out the way forward together, this soon becomes obvious, no matter what the form of the conversation.

It is about balance and, in many situations, this balance comes down to professional judgement and developing adaptive expertise. The features of the conversations described in this chapter are designed to develop this balance where those involved trust the openness of those leading them, respect their expertise and their role in promoting professional learning and practice improvements, and accept that challenge is an integral part of the process.

Plan professional conversations

Planning conversations may seem unnecessary at first, but as knowledge of the power of these co-constructed conversations deepens, the importance of planning becomes evident. It also becomes easier as metacognitive awareness of conversational strategies deepens.

The planning prompts that follow can assist leaders to develop more effective professional conversations. The prompts include aspects such as the purpose and focus of the conversation; anticipated knowledge, dispositions and vulnerabilities; the context in which the conversation takes place; and the relationships and resources that may enhance learning.

Purpose and focus

Issues around purpose and focus were described at the beginning of this chapter. Purpose and focus in professional conversations help avoid confusion and promote trust, and ideally should be balanced alongside flexibility and consultation. These prompts and others come together by thinking about:

> What professional learning do I want to promote in consultation with the participant(s)?

- Do I need to check this prior to the meeting?
- Have we agreed on previous actions that need to be reviewed?

Anticipated knowledge, dispositions and vulnerabilities

In planning a conversation, it is important to clarify:

> What are the strengths, challenges and vulnerabilities of the participant that I need to acknowledge and build on?
> Am I aware of the assumptions I am bringing to the conversation?

Buried and untested assumptions will form a subtext in the conversation and shape it if they are not unearthed and examined. In a conversation with a particular person or team, assumptions that may need to be checked or prompt thinking about what is anticipated include those about the other participant's:

- level of actionable knowledge in the area of focus
- commitment to moral purpose and curiosity
- beliefs about teaching and leadership
- professional aspirations
- mindset and attitudes to their own learning and that of others.

It is also useful to consider any other aspects in which you as the leader of the conversation might feel vulnerable.

On the surface, strengths look easy to reveal and check, but assumptions are often made about the limitations of someone's knowledge that are unfounded. It is important to listen carefully to ensure participants have the knowledge needed to interpret a given situation and make appropriate improvements.

Context

We tend to think of context as primary, secondary, rural, metropolitan, etc. but these kinds of categorisations do not reveal the nuances of context that need to be considered in professional conversations. In reflecting on context, questions to ask yourself include:

What's going on for the participant(s)?
What assumptions do I need to identify and check in terms of their current reality?

Considerations about contexts include:

- health and wellbeing
- experience of the other person(s)
- timing in terms of other commitments
- relationships in the group and within the school/organisation
- who initiated the conversation and why?

As with assumptions about knowledge, dispositions and vulnerabilities, this planning process is about unearthing assumptions about context to identify what to check and not to presuppose that your assumptions are correct.

Relationships

Relationships here refer to relationships between the person leading the conversation and the other participant(s), rather than relationships among team members (which is addressed in the context). Questions to ask yourself about relationships include:

> To what extent do we have a relationship of trust and mutual respect?

- To what extent does this relationship include challenging beliefs and practice?
- Do I need to increase or decrease this level of challenge?
- What is likely to be the future relationship?

Resources

Resources refer to the evidence needed to inform the conversation, the artefacts needed to shape it and the expertise available to promote learning. These 3 resources come together to complement the purpose. Questions to ask yourself in preparation include:

> Do I have the right resources to support the professional learning focus?

- What kind of evidence would be most informative for the purpose of this conversation?
- Do I need supporting artefacts that will help promote learning around this purpose?
- Will the right expertise be in the room to promote learning in ways that will enhance outcomes for students?

These planning prompts and the relevant questions and considerations are also reproduced in a corresponding template with space for notes that is included in the supplementary digital resources (see p. 116).

Analyse your conversations

As mentioned in Chapter 1, reading about conversations typically leads to little improvement. You also need to practise and analyse your own conversations formatively so you can identify what you do well and what needs work. The steps in this process involve:

1. Preparation
   - Decide which strategies are most useful for you to focus on as a personal professional learning goal in conversations.
   - Use the supplementary planning framework template to think about how you will approach the conversation.
   - Identify an educator with whom you can practise, explain the process and seek their permission.
2. Recording and analysis
   - Record the first 10-15 minutes of the conversation and convert it to a transcript using a voice-to-text function.
   - Analyse the focus features of your conversation with your colleagues using the criteria below, then consider the transcript overall in terms of the attributes of adaptive expertise.
3. Reflection
   - Seek feedback from colleagues and the person with whom you practised this conversation.
   - Decide what further reading and practice you need to master the strategies you have focused on or move to a more demanding focus.

Criteria for analysis

As anyone familiar with formative assessment principles knows, any assessment, but particularly self-assessment, is enhanced by the articulation of success criteria. The evidence, in this case a recording of your conversation, can be self-assessed using the criteria and a professional learning goal focused on aspects to practise further.

Criteria based on the material in this 'Getting started' chapter are summarised in Figure 2.2, with a reminder of why each is important. The criteria were developed in conjunction with groups of regional and school leaders. They may not all apply to a particular conversation, and it is important that the ones considered relevant to the context are selected. The criteria are included under the headings: 'Transparency in the process', 'Building actionable knowledge', 'Relationships' and 'Resources'. A template repeating the criteria in Figure 2.2, with space added for evidence from your conversation transcript is included in the supplementary digital resources (see p. 116).

Transparency in the process

Shared understanding of purpose and process, with all participants able to express, engage and test different ideas through deep inquiry, enriches conversations and builds commitment to change.

- Clear purpose and process negotiated with participants
- Beliefs and reasoning expressed in ways that invite others to express their beliefs
- Genuine inquiry and curiosity evident by all participants, with questions accompanied by reasons (including those around the evidence)
- Evidence of professional practice linked to the outcomes of that practice
- Moral purpose around student learning used as a touchstone at critical points in the conversation

Building actionable knowledge

New actionable knowledge and a strong moral purpose is fundamental to change and improvement in student outcomes.

- Evidence of actionable knowledge building (what and how)
- Evidence of commitment to acting on that knowledge (unpacking what that might mean in practice)

Relationships

Relationships of trust and mutual respect need to be accompanied by challenge and high expectations for the conversations to lead to improvement.

- Relationships of trust and mutual respect evident (maintaining relationships)
- Relationships include challenge and high expectations in order to have more of an impact

Resources

The resources brought to conversations shape the quality and direction of the conversation. The 3 main categories are artefacts, expertise and evidence.

- Artefacts or documentation relevant to the particular conversation used to promote professional learning (e.g. progressions in PLCs; frameworks for effective meetings)
- Expertise specific to the focus of the conversation (e.g. curriculum or pedagogical expertise)
- Evidence of learner progress linked to professional practice; learner progress may refer to students or teachers depending on the context of the conversation:
  - progress of student learners (e.g. formal assessments or observations) linked to evidence of changes in teaching practice
  - progress of teacher learners (e.g. changes in professional understanding or practice) linked to changes in leadership practice

FIGURE 2.2 Criteria for effective conversations in promoting professional learning

An important feature of complexity is that the parts do not necessarily add up to the whole (Cochran-Smith et al. 2014). When this idea is applied to professional learning conversations, meeting all the above criteria may not realise the goal of developing adaptive expertise. Part of the analysis process, therefore, needs to include a more overall judgement about the extent to which your approach to professional conversations is contributing to developing this expertise. The key questions and attributes are listed below. There is also a corresponding template in the supplementary digital resources (see p. 116) that lists the attributes and provides space for reflection on each.

The key questions are:

- To what extent did I demonstrate these attributes?
- To what extent did I develop these attributes in the person with whom I was having the conversation?

The attributes of adaptive expertise include:

- thinking and acting evaluatively about impact on student outcomes
- seeking deep knowledge to make more of a difference
- thinking metacognitively
- working collaboratively
- thinking and acting responsively
- thinking and acting systemically.

After working with the criteria, engaging with colleagues in the analysis process, and reflecting on the effectiveness of your conversations, it is time to deepen your learning by moving on to the strategies described in Chapter 3.

CHAPTER 3
Going deeper

Introduction

Chapter 3 builds on the material in the previous chapter by 'going deeper'. The strategies in this chapter are designed to delve into the complexity typical of education environments and, therefore, further develop adaptive expertise. The strategies and conversation examples provided to illustrate them include the features identified in Figure 3.1.

FIGURE 3.1 Features of conversations described in Chapter 3: Going deeper

The format of the sections in the chapter is similar to that of Chapter 2. Each feature is described with the underpinning rationale, illustrated by conversation examples and accompanied by thinking prompts.

Build theoretical knowledge through practice

Professional conversations designed to improve practice and student outcomes usually involve developing educational knowledge. In Chapter 2, the emphasis was on building actionable knowledge. Actionable knowledge focuses on knowing 'what' and 'how'. However, to understand how to transfer this practical knowledge to a variety of contexts, knowing 'why' is as important. Knowing 'why' facilitates its transfer and the knowledge becomes theoretical. Pellegrino and Hilton (2012) define deep knowledge as transferrable knowledge. This deep knowledge also underpins adaptive expertise because, in order to act responsively to a given context, educators need to be able to draw on deep pedagogical, curriculum and leadership knowledge.

Sometimes the idea of theory is interpreted as being able to quote a given researcher. The 'theory' I mean here refers to the concepts and thinking underpinning particular practices. Unless this thinking is unpacked, such references to research do not deepen theoretical knowledge. The person enacting the practice needs to know why this researcher advocates doing things this way and not some other way. What is the theory behind it? What evidence is it based on?

Knowing 'what' and 'how' is useful in building situation-specific practice. Deeper theoretical understanding facilitates the transfer of new knowledge from one situation to another and how it can be adapted to realise a wider purpose. For example, many states have inquiry improvement cycles. If they are seen as a discrete set of steps, then the potential richness and challenge involved in inquiry approaches to professional learning are likely to be missed, with limited outcomes realised. Inquiry improvement cycles could, instead, be seen in more systemic terms, as a way to challenge current thinking and practice, and as an opportunity to deepen understanding holistically about what is leading to a particular situation. The potential richness is then more likely to be addressed. The chances of success increase together with the development of adaptive expertise.

💡 THINKING PROMPTS
- Have I explained 'why', as well as 'what' and 'how'?
- Do others now understand the 'why'?
- How do I know?

Many of the strategies described in Chapter 2 sought to develop more theoretical knowledge through leaders elaborating their thinking. In the following example, a team leader gives practical descriptions of students' limited understanding of part–whole in numeracy. The team leader situates that knowledge within the bigger picture of mathematical operations. When painting this kind of 'bigger picture' becomes habitual in conversations, leaders and teachers broaden their horizons about how the specifics of a particular skill are situated within a broader theoretical idea.

Earlier in this conversation, the team leader (TL) had encouraged the teacher (T) to help young students to understand part–whole by splitting numbers up.

T: Yes, I probably wouldn't mind doing some activities with partitioning of numbers and just looking at some different numbers and breaking them into parts flexibly, to give them more of an idea of the parts that can go together to make a number. A few of the kids, I showed them the 3 and 4 and put them together to make 7 and when I asked them to split it into parts, they would just make it into 3 and 4 again and that was sort of the only way because that was what they'd seen. So, I think that extending that would help them as well.

TL: And the research says that if kids can pull numbers apart and manipulate them, they're going to be okay with their operations and their maths becomes a good, solid foundation to build on.

One way to build more theoretical understanding is to habitually provide the reasons for making comments or giving advice, whether to another leader about leadership or a teacher about teaching. These reasons help educators make connections between the specifics of practice and the underpinning theoretical ideas.

This next example is a conversation between a regional leader (RL) and a school principal (SP). During the regional leader's previous visit to the school, the principal had expressed frustration at the limited changes in teaching and learning that they had been promoting and expecting. The principal revealed that they were trying to shift the culture of the school through multiple initiatives but were not getting the traction they anticipated. The regional leader had mentioned on a previous occasion that doing too much typically leads to little real change. A more likely outcome was exhausted staff. For this reason, the regional leader had advocated reducing the number of initiatives in the school and going much deeper with the 2 that remained.

SP: What I'm thinking about now is our planning. We didn't get a lot of traction last term so after talking to you, we've got only 2 priorities: deep learning and PBL [Positive Behaviour for Learning] for behaviour. So, when you look at it, it looks sharp and skinny, but there's still actually quite a lot going on.

We've unpacked deep learning and we've narrowed that down for now into collaborative learning, focused instruction, guided instruction and independent learning. We've developed resources and I've made a short video for each that the teachers can watch. They can choose when they do this. Some do it in their PLCs; others prefer to watch them in their own time if there are other priorities for the PLC. We also have staff meeting time, of course, but sometimes we need to talk about other things because there is so much happening that the department wants us to cover. In the PLCs, they are also using the spiral of inquiry. Some are using that for PBL.

RL: I talked last time about reducing the number of initiatives and having them come together into a coherent schooling improvement and professional learning plan that includes both the focus for change and the forums where that happens. As we discussed last time, there is a lot of research telling us that doing less and doing it well is more effective than doing a lot of things superficially. There is still a lot of new learning for teachers in each of those areas. It may still be too much. Do you have any evidence about what changes are actually happening and how the teachers are feeling?

[*Reiterates theory of change with respect to too many initiatives and limited traction, and the need for a coherent plan*]

SP: Not yet. We have only been working on this skinny version for just over a term. I know lots of teachers have watched the videos. They seem to be going down well.

RL: OK. One term in. Hmm. We talked last time about having an overall plan because this can give clarity to everyone about where you are heading and how things fit together. Clarity reduces uncertainty and you are more likely to get people committed.

[*The purpose for the plan is to give clarity and reduce uncertainty; articulates underpinning theory*]

SP: Not yet. I've got a PBL plan and one for deep learning. We've had spirals of inquiry and PLCs for a while so they should be humming along by now.

RL: I'd like to spend some time with you mapping out how things fit together, including collecting evidence about what is working for whom right now – rather than just going ahead with the rollout of each of these plans separately. It may be too early to get shifts in student learning, but it is important to collect ongoing evidence from your middle leaders and the teachers about how they see things fitting together, so you are getting feedback about how things are travelling. It's just like formative feedback in classes. How are the teachers feeling about the expected changes? What is their level of understanding and commitment to PBL and deep learning? Without this ongoing evaluative evidence, you are flying blind.

> [Draws a parallel between formative feedback (which the principal knows about) and checking progress at the organisational level; provides clear reasons for suggestions]

SP: I don't want all this to come to a grinding halt. It's important we keep moving forward. We've cut back a lot so this should be manageable.

RL: Hopefully; I'm not suggesting coming to a grinding halt. Manageability can only be decided by asking those responsible for the implementation. What I am suggesting is that we develop a map of how these 2 big initiatives are coming together in your different professional learning forums. You've got PLCs and spirals of inquiry, staff meetings and individual learning. I wonder how the staff see those fitting together. Unless they can see the coherence that you see, they are likely to disengage because it just looks like more and more of separate bits. When we've got the map, we need to work out how you will get some evidence about the changes that are, or are not, happening.

> [Reiterates the importance of coherence, clarity and engagement, with evidence to check]

SP: I really get a sense of enthusiasm from everyone.

RL: That's great. Enthusiasm is central to change, but we need the map first to identify what they are enthusiastic about and what they are having problems with. Is that ok?

SP: [principal indicates agreement] I think I could put a map together and give it to the others. That might help them.

RL: You referred to collaboration as part of your deep learning. Collaboration occurs through all layers of a school if it is to be consistent in its values. This seems to me to be the time to bring in your senior and middle leaders to develop the map together because this will help them to understand your thinking and for you to get some feedback from them about what they are thinking and finding.

A collaboratively developed plan and map is much more powerful in creating change. How does that feel to you?

[*Draws parallels between leading, teaching and learning to illustrate the theoretical point*]

SP: They have been on this journey with me all the way through, but I guess it has been largely directed by me. We could invite them in for next time.

The regional leader noted in reflections on this transcript that the principal still did not 'own' the ideas put forward and that their preference was to develop the map and give it to the other leaders. The principal understood that doing too much was likely to lead to limited change and an exhausted staff but was convinced that the 2 initiatives were manageable for them. Rather than argue about this point, the regional leader decided that checking both their views by gathering evidence and working together to see the process as feedback for the principal, would be more likely to lead to change. As is often the case, more than one conversation was needed to create the shifts in thinking and leadership practice.

Ladder of inference

As with any profession, teaching and leading involve constant interpretations of what is observed, with moment-by-moment decisions made on the basis of these observations. Throughout this book, I emphasise the use of evidence, but evidence can be interpreted in many ways. Some see evidence through a lens of a glass half full. Others see the same evidence through a lens of a glass half empty and arrive at different conclusions. Some want to confirm their own point of view, so they attend to the aspects of the evidence that are consistent with that viewpoint. Others attend to different aspects of the evidence and interpret it accordingly. These different foci are likely to lead to different interpretations and conclusions.

Argyris (1982) developed the ladder of inference to represent how we reason from evidence. The ladder of inference has become a widely used artefact to help slow down reasoning from evidence and to help those involved in a conversation move onto the same page. The ladder of inference describes how everyone reasons. In complex environments, like those in education settings, there is always a multitude of possible evidence that could be attended to. From this complexity, we select evidence, then describe that evidence, leading to its interpretation and subsequent conclusions. Sometimes this process occurs so rapidly we go straight to the conclusions without being aware we have raced up the ladder of inference. For example, after attending a staff meeting where the views of one staff member were different from those of the principal, those in attendance may come to very different conclusions, without being aware of the difference in evidence they have drawn on and how they have interpreted it. Some who disagree with the staff member may say, 'The principal handled that well'. Others who agreed with the staff member are more likely to think, 'The principal shut that down unnecessarily'. Both race to the top of the ladder without carefully unpacking the evidence they have drawn on, how they interpreted it and the conclusions they reached.

In complex situations, typical of education, there are usually many possible interpretations and conclusions for any set of evidence, whether the evidence is in numerical student scores about achievement, survey results or observed interactions between educators or their students. In situations where there is potential disagreement, it is important to work systematically from the evidence to the interpretations to the conclusions, to make sure all those involved are on the same 'ladder of inference' (see Figure 3.2). This way, everyone is focused on the same evidence, describes it in the similar ways, negotiates possible

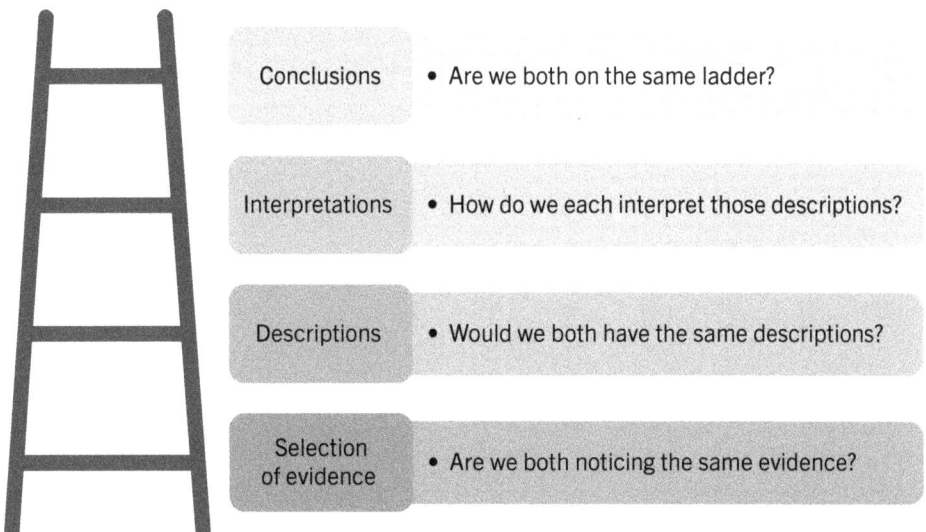

FIGURE 3.2 The ladder of inference

interpretations and draws similar conclusions. This deliberate process helps to develop relational trust and adaptive expertise.

While evidence may take multiple forms, observations of practice are particularly fraught, with the possibility of multiple interpretations and conclusions. For this reason, observations should start at the bottom of the ladder by being explicit about the pool of data or evidence selected in a given situation. Imagine observing in a classroom. There are many possibilities to focus on, including the physical layout, the resources used, the difficulty level of resources, teacher movements around the classroom, teachers' interactions with students and students' interactions with one another. The first potential point of difference is the evidence selected for attention. The observer might focus on the 5 off-task students seated at the back. The teacher, on the other hand, might be focusing on the group with whom they are working. The descriptions of what is happening are very different. Then, these descriptions become interpreted. Sometimes this interpretation process is referred to as having a 'hunch'. The observer is concerned about the students being off task and has a hunch that the resources are too difficult and the pace of the lesson is too fast. The teacher, on the other hand, is relieved that the group they are working with are highly engaged and have learned a new concept. Each draws different conclusions about the effectiveness of the lesson.

Even when both observer and teacher focus on the same evidence and describe it in the same way, they still may draw different conclusions. For example, if both focus on the 5 off-task students, their off-task behaviour may be interpreted in different ways. The teacher may blame the students for being unmotivated and disengaged. The observer may focus on the appropriateness of the resources provided and the pace of the lesson. As a result, different conclusions are drawn.

💡 THINKING PROMPTS
- Have I explained the evidence I noticed, how I described and interpreted it and the conclusions I drew from it?
- Have I asked the other person to do the same?

To illustrate how this might work in a real situation, this next conversation between a team leader (TL) and teacher (T) is focused on a shared concern about a young student, Jordan, who was having difficulties with their writing. The team leader became concerned about a perceived mismatch between the learning intention and the teaching sequence that was supposed to focus on structure, and how that led to Jordan failing to write anything. The teacher, on the other hand, had little expectation that Jordan would write anything so did not perceive that the mismatch contributed to Jordan's difficulties. The students were learning about the structure of a recount by retelling the story of *Goldilocks and the 3 bears*.

TL: So, you started with the structure of a beginning, middle and end in your lesson introduction. The kids did a think/pair/share about that, but then you went on to describe Goldilocks. I was puzzled why you did that because the learning intention was to do a beginning, middle and end and to use time connectives. I'm interested in your thinking around that.
> [*Makes evidence and description explicit at the bottom of the ladder of inference; inquires into the teachers' thinking*]

T: It was my initial decision to describe the beginning, middle and end of the sequence in *Goldilocks and the 3 bears*. In the story, Goldilocks was an innocent; just wandered into the house. It could be that she wasn't so innocent. Should she have done that? I wanted them to think about that. Rather than just saying 'Goldilocks', I wanted to get them to describe her as they saw her.

TL: Okay

T: What kind of girl was she? Just to add more character into their writing, even though it wasn't part of my learning intention.

TL: Okay, so I think I'm understanding why you did that now because initially I thought, 'Oh, I wonder why he's making that decision to stop and describe Goldilocks. Because the learning intention was about the beginning, middle, end.'
> [*Makes interpretation explicit*]

T: That's right. I just thought they're at the point now where I don't want them to just say, 'Goldilocks'. Or 'the father bear'. We're going to go deeper in the writing and give more information to the audience rather than just writing 'Goldilocks went for a walk' or 'The bears came home'.

TL: You wanted more information, although the learning intention was about beginning, middle, end. As you know, I was there to observe

>   Jordan and we know this student's challenges. So, I'd like to unpack what was happening in the lesson and what the impact on Jordan appeared to be.
>
>   *[Links to conclusions about what was happening for Jordan]*

T: Yes

TL: And so, what I observed … Firstly, I thought there was a lot going on in that lesson. And so, is it okay if I just tell you all the things that you did in that lesson?

>   *[Gives interpretation (third 'rung' of ladder of inference): 'a lot going on'; then goes back down the ladder (first 'rung' – evidence)]*

T: Yes, go for it

TL: Now it might be a bit confronting, but I think it's important because I've been you. I've been that person that's tried to fit everything into the lesson.

T: Yes.

TL: And just while I'm telling you all the things that you put in the lesson, just imagine you're one of the kids. Imagine you're Jordan. Okay, so in that lesson you started off with what happened in the story, so a recap. Then you started asking them what happened in the beginning, middle and end and you did that with the think/pair/share.

>   *[Provides interpretation: 'imagine you're Jordan'; presents evidence: description of lesson]*

T: Yes.

TL: Then you went on to describe Goldilocks and asked, 'So tell me about Goldilocks'. Then you went back to modelling how to do the plan for the beginning, middle and end. Then you also told them that you're going to use time connectives and then you stopped to ask, 'What is a time connective?' So you spent a bit of time discussing what a time connective is. Then you showed them how to rule up their book. And you went step 1, step 2, step 3, so your instructions were very explicit. And then you told them what the success criteria were. So, 'I want you to use time connectives' and then you … just said to them, 'Just write what happens in the beginning, middle and end'. And then you sent them off. So that's about 7 things that you included in one lesson.

[*Gives description of evidence noticed at the bottom of the ladder of inference to be clear what evidence was drawn on to make inferences and conclusions*]

T: Yes, sounds like a lot but I didn't want the kids to be bored and beginnings, middle and ends can be boring.

[*Reveals own theories of practice*]

TL: So, I was watching Jordan, who didn't even get started. Did you notice?

[*Checks what evidence was being noticed*]

T: No. I assume Jordan didn't write anything.

The differences between the team leader and teacher with respect to the evidence and descriptions they attended to, the inferences they made and the conclusions they drew are summarised in Figure 3.3.

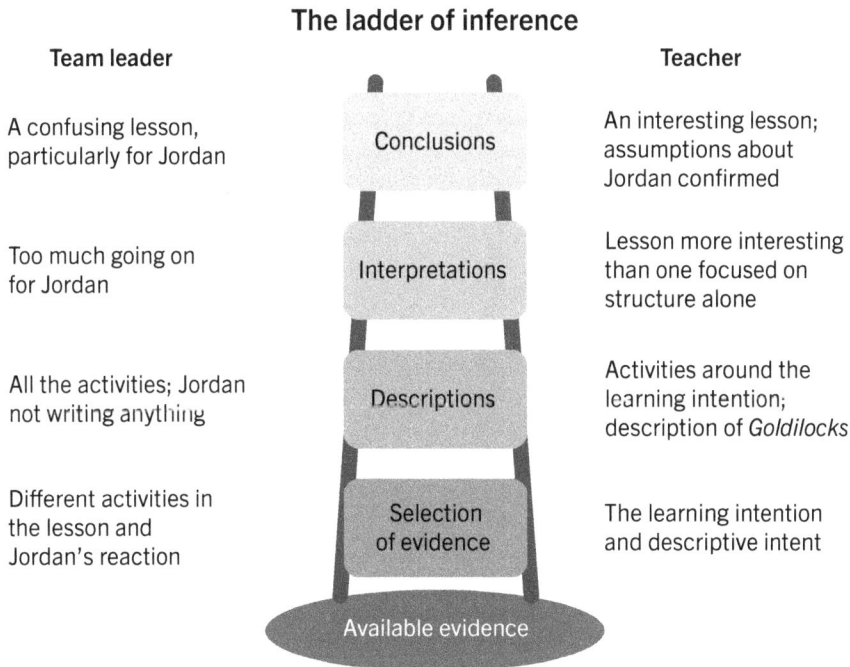

FIGURE 3.3 The ladder of inference for the team leader and teacher

The careful movement up the ladder of inference, from the evidence noticed to the description and interpretation of that evidence, enabled the leader and the teacher to understand their different interpretations and conclusions. Further on in the conversation, these differences were reconciled.

An example of the ladder of inference populated with prompt questions is provided in the supplementary digital resources, along with a template on which to fill in both the other participants' reasoning and your own (see p. 116).

Unpack theories of practice

In Chapter 2, one of the illustrated features of conversations involved probing for beliefs underpinning particular practices in order to understand differences in viewpoints. This probing should not be for the purpose of persuasion, because that undermines trust. Rather, the purpose should be to understand where each viewpoint is coming from. Unpacking theories of practice takes this feature a step further, to being more systematic about connecting beliefs and actions, together with the consequences of those actions. The reason for identifying consequences is because they typically form the catalyst for change when they are not the consequences desired.

When unpacking a theory of action, it is important to start with the actions themselves, for example, a particular teaching or leadership practice. Then work with the participant to identify the beliefs and values underpinning those particular actions. Some beliefs may be about effective teaching or leading, others may be about something entirely different. Through this process, the participants may find their own beliefs are in tension with each other, thus creating dilemmas. A standard dilemma for leaders is a belief about the need for the improvement of teaching and learning, and a competing belief about the importance of positive relationships with staff when desired change is not happening. The dilemma becomes how to give the improvement messages while maintaining positive relationships. This dilemma can often be resolved by working through theories of practice and is improved considerably when consequences are explicitly identified.

Therefore, the next step is to unpack the consequences for the leader and those educators or students for whom the leader has responsibility. Some of these consequences are intended; many are unintended. To follow through the above example of the dilemma between improvement and relationships, often the relationship is prioritised over clear messages about expectations of change. The leader's actions usually involve giving the teacher indirect but supportive messages about the need for change, with the consequences typically becoming superficial change without the depth intended.

💡 THINKING PROMPTS
- Have I asked about the other person's beliefs, which led to their actions, or have I assumed I know?
- Have we agreed on the consequences of the other person's actions, or have these remained unstated?

In the following example, a school principal (SP) was working with a senior leader (SL) of a large secondary school. The senior leader commented frequently that they were feeling stressed by the amount of work involved in running the curriculum team on top of their other leadership responsibilities. They complained that a team leader, Casey, who attended team meetings was negative, blocking ideas and constantly making blanket statements about why something wouldn't work. It was agreed that to find a way through, the principal should attend the team meeting and observe what was happening. This was framed as an opportunity for leadership development for the senior leader. In this follow-up conversation, this framing, together with explicit reference to theories of practice, helped the senior leader to develop their leadership skills.

SP: Tell me what was going on for you during the meeting, so I get an idea of the dynamics with the team leader.
   [*Provides a reason for the request; inquires into thinking*]

SL: I guess I'm feeling quite jaded in that I'm the one, me, I'm the one that's leading the work; I'm the one that creates the activities; I'm the one that takes the notes from the meeting. No-one else does much. Casey [team leader] puts the chairs out.

SP: OK, I noticed that.
   [*Demonstrates they notice the same evidence on the ladder of inference*]

SL: You know, I think Casey doesn't bring much to the meeting and always has a negative attitude. Whereas Chanda and I get excited about what we're doing.

SP: Yes, I get that. And I suppose just like you've got a range of students in any class, as a school leader we're thinking about how we can get

that commitment from everyone we lead. It's hard. I'd like to focus on your leadership for a while.
[*Brings the focus back to the agreed agenda of leadership development*]

SL: My confidence has been growing. I'm in my second year now and last year I was so unsure, but now I feel I've definitely found my feet. Casey and the others are really challenging me, but I feel I'm much better placed to be driving things and putting my opinion forward and that sort of thing.

SP: So, the challenge now is thinking, 'I don't have to do everything'. So, let's work on how you can change that dynamic.

It is often helpful to create a theory of action diagram that summarises beliefs, actions and consequences. Always start by identifying the actions; what the educator actually did that is observable. Both the principal and the senior leader were able to agree that the leader's key actions involved driving the meeting, together with the original complaint of 'doing all the work'.

Then, consider the beliefs, values or any other issues that shape those actions. This leader clearly had strong views about confident leadership as is evident in the above conversation.

The third step is to identify the consequences of the actions. Again, the senior leader had identified these in the conversation prior to the meeting. The order in which the 3 components are presented in the final diagram, however, is different from the order in which they are identified, because beliefs drive actions, and the consequences are a result of the action. The theory of action for the senior leader is summarised in Figure 3.4.

The sketched diagram serves at least 2 purposes. It invites those participating in the conversation to elaborate and fill in missing parts of the situation and so helps to develop a shared picture of what is leading to what. It helps the participants to see the causal patterns – What I think and do leads to particular consequences. What a leader thinks and does is, of course, influenced by what others think and do. This is not a blame game. It gives an insight into potential levers for change. Changing the actions in order to change the consequences is likely to challenge beliefs.

In this second, more complex example, a regional leader and secondary school principal were working with an associate principal to resolve an issue with a senior

Beliefs and values

As a leader my job is to:
- drive things
- put opinions forward.

Actions resulting from those

When leading meetings, the actions I take are to:
- drive the meeting
- do all the work.

Consequences of the actions

As a result:
- there is lack of commitment from others
- team members demonstrate blocking and negativity
- I feel jaded.

FIGURE 3.4 The school leader's theory of action

school leader who apparently was not undertaking the tasks associated with their staffing role. The regional leader (RL) is showing the associate principal (AP) how to map a theory of action to develop an understanding of the problem and to lead to its resolution.

RL: From our previous conversation, I understood that there are issues with some of your senior leaders and difficulties in developing them as school leaders that you would like to resolve. Would you be able to give me a bit of context about that to help me understand what is happening? Thanks.

[*Clearly states the purpose and reason for requesting information*]

AP: Yes. So, currently, at the school, out of the 6 senior leaders that I am responsible for leading, 3 of them have also started their teaching career here at the school. So, they don't have life experiences, or other experiences to bring to the table. All of our senior leaders have an operational school-wide role, as well as leading a faculty.

RL: You mentioned in a previous conversation that there was one particular leader that you wanted to focus on. Could you tell me a little bit more about that leader? Just in terms of what their roles are within the school.

[Provides reason for asking for information]

AP: Yes. So, Chen is one of the ones who started their teaching career as a new educator at the school, and therefore has limited other experiences to bring to the table. However, the faculty that Chen started in was well run. The previous leader had high expectations and was able to relay that to the staff in her faculty. So, Chen has been brought up under that model and does a good job. But also, developing some of it even further, to make sure that the faculty is running at a very high level, meets all of the deadlines, delivering innovative pedagogy in classrooms. Instructional leadership is happening.

The challenge, however, has been in the school-wide role, which is technical; so it is around staffing. So, it's quite a technical role.

RL: So, is that one of the areas where you would like to develop your leadership capabilities? To be able to work with Chen to lead the staffing team?

[Keeps the focus on the stated learning purpose for the meeting]

AP: Yes.

RL: Okay. So, can you tell me about some of the actions that you're currently undertaking to support Chen in that staffing realm, to help develop as an effective leader.

[Begins identifying actions; first step in drawing a theory of action]

AP: So, with the staffing role, it is so technical, that if you have not been in the role, or exposed to that role before, it can be quite daunting. When you don't know what questions to ask, you actually don't know what you're meant to be doing. So, what I have found in our current situation is that because I have knowledge and experience, as a previous staffing officer, that I am tending to do a lot of the jobs myself.

RL: Okay, so you feel you're increasing your workload. I get a sense of frustration from you.

AP: Yes, that's absolutely right.

RL: Can you tell me of any other actions that you've currently put into place to support Chen, perhaps other than, you know, doing parts of the role yourself?
    [*Probes for additional actions*]

AP: So, one of the strategies I put into place was a weekly catch-up meeting, where I asked Chen to come with questions. And I presented myself as a support person. So, to come to me with questions that they needed answers for and as a person who has done the stuff in that role for a number of years, I will be able to teach or demonstrate what needs to be done.

RL: And these particular questions, how have you guided Chen through those questions? Would you be able to tell me a bit more about that?
    [*Reasons for regional leader's questions implied from the conversation so far*]

AP: So, one of the things that I was hoping for was that Chen would be able to take the initiative, and may have already done some research into 'What does the staffing role in a school look like?' and 'What might my role be? However, what I have found is that when Chen comes to the meetings, and I ask what questions there are for me, the answer is, 'I don't have any'. And when I point out that there has to be questions because at the moment, I'm still doing so many of the staffing tasks, I get back, 'Well, I don't know what it is. So therefore, I don't know what questions to ask'. So, Chen's not learning to do the job.

RL: I'm constructing this diagram of what is going on [theory of action], and I want to make sure I have captured the main actions you have taken. It seems firstly, you are doing the tasks yourself, so they get done. Secondly, you have a weekly catch-up meeting so Chen can ask questions about the staffing role. Are those the main things?

AP: [indicates agreement]

RL: And the consequences here are you have increased your workload and you are feeling frustrated Chen isn't learning to do the job.
    [*Is open about the process; identifies consequences revealed so far*]

AP: Yes, that's right and it's been happening all year.

RL: Let's unpack the consequences a bit more. Any other consequences for either yourself or Chen? Positive or negative?

AP: While I'm still doing Chen's job, I feel that as a senior leader, I'm not doing my job in being able to help someone else do theirs. Chen's not going to learn if I continue to do the job myself. Is that making sense?

[Identifies additional consequences]

RL: Yes, it is.

AP: But it does mean that Chen has a lot more time to spend on developing instructional leadership capability and doing lots of lesson observations. So, pedagogy in the classroom is definitely happening. However, the school-wide role at the moment is not happening and Chen isn't taking ownership of it. I would like to see Chen actually own the fact that there are 2 parts of this job and to take some initiative, to at least try and figure out what the role looks like and what Chen's part in it is, and then maybe be accountable and make some decisions around where to next.

RL: OK. I've summarised that in the consequences box here. Let's go up here to the beliefs. From what you have said you believe that leaders should take the initiative to develop the knowledge to do their job. Is that right?

[Is open about the process]

AP: Well of course it is, they are paid to be a leader.

RL: Are there any other beliefs you have that have led to you working with Chen in this way?

AP: Well as [secondary school principal] here knows, I have high expectations of all the leaders and expect them to perform their roles. Neither of us has any credibility if someone you are responsible for doesn't do their job.

RL: So, credibility is something you are really concerned about. I just want to check I've got this right before we move onto how to solve it. I think there is a real opportunity for leadership development for you in this. Thanks for being so honest.

The completed theory of action diagram is summarised in Figure 3.5.

Beliefs and values

- Leaders should take the initiative to develop the knowledge to do the job they are paid for.
- I have high expectations of leaders and failure of someone I have responsibility for to do their job reflects on my credibility as an associate principal.

Actions resulting from those

- I do the job myself when others don't do the job.
- I organise weekly catch-up meeting with opportunities for Chen to ask questions.

Consequences of the actions

- There is an increase in my workload.
- I'm frustrated Chen isn't doing all of their job.
- I'm feeling a failure in not doing my job because I haven't been able to help Chen do their job.
- Chen has time to be an effective instructional leader but is not taking ownership of the staffing part of their job.

FIGURE 3.5 The associate principal's theory of action

The mapping of the theory of action then led to identifying alternative preferred consequences and how the associate principal's leadership actions would need to change to realise these alternatives. The principal of the school agreed to work with the associate principal on this issue and a number of similar leadership challenges that had arisen in the associate principal's role.

A template for completing a theory of action for your own conversation is provided in the supplementary digital resources (see p. 116).

Agree on the problem before the solution

Action is central to the work of educators. The job involves constantly taking action to resolve complex challenges. But the nature of complex challenges means they typically have multiple causes and are characterised by interactions and interdependencies, as described in Chapter 1. Some may see problems where others consider it to be just how things happen. Different participants in a conversation often have different ideas about the existence of a problem, the possible causes, and therefore, the best solution. Inquiry cycles are usually built around the idea of developing a shared analysis before developing strategies to meet these complex challenges. It is therefore important to agree on the nature of the challenge and its possible causes before deciding on strategies to improve the situation. This is the essence of genuine inquiry described in Chapter 2.

The ladder of inference and identifying theories of action are both strategies that contribute to developing a shared understanding of problems or challenges. As illustrated in the section on the ladder of inference, different participants may notice different evidence and interpret it through a different lens. The theory of action scenario identifies how actions and beliefs may contribute to a particular challenge. The purpose of both strategies is to provide an analysis of a situation and to use evidence in ways that capture the differing personal theories, with an agreed process for deciding on a course of action.

In this next scenario, a Year 7 team leader (TL) is discussing the limited progress in the team's inquiry with a senior school leader (SL). The school had inquiry teams for each year level. The team leader had invited the senior school leader to attend the meeting and help to diagnose why the group appeared to be experiencing this roadblock after their initial enthusiasm. The senior school leader had scanned websites for tools to help the team leader to get back on track. This example begins some time into the conversation when the difficulties had been acknowledged but not analysed.

TL: Perhaps, our team is still adapting to or getting used to the inquiry spiral and not being able to skip straight ahead to look at tools and strategies and really jumping into it. It's great to have that enthusiasm to improve student learning but I don't think we're targeting the right sorts of things. We're not honing in on a specific skill and also building our own practice around being able to cater for the students in a particular skill. It feels too rushed, but everyone wants to get on with it.

[*Shows awareness of the problem but is unsure what gave rise to it apart from 'getting used to the inquiry spiral'*]

SL: Yes, I suppose that would be what I really noticed. You seemed as a team to be at a bit of a roadblock as to where you need to go next. You want to capitalise on the enthusiasm, but it doesn't seem you have done enough groundwork to move forward together. What I'm noticing across lots of the inquiry teams is that everyone is jumping ahead too quickly to come up with lots of strategies rather than diagnosing what's happening for learners. I'm not sure if it's a sense of urgency or that we are time-bound to the end of the year or what it is.

TL: I'm worried if we slow down, I'll lose the enthusiasm.

SL: Yes, teachers are used to 'doing something' when they can see a problem. In many ways it's the nature of teaching. But I think you will lose enthusiasm, and probably already have, by not really making much progress together.

The inquiry spiral is designed to interrupt the 'doing something' by finding out what is going on for learners. And it comes down to lots of teacher learning, which the teachers may not be aware of.

[Acknowledges the team leader's dilemma; identifies the theory behind the resource]

TL: Yes, that would be accurate. Yes.

SL: Let's unpack a bit about what might be leading to the roadblock. From what I observed, you administered a pre-test to find out what the students knew but it seemed to me the team didn't know what to do with the results. I suppose my thinking was, 'Did you do enough work on the early stages of the spiral?' So as a team, did you spend some time actually unpacking the curriculum and looking at the questions? Do you have a shared understanding of what the results of the pre-test told you? Is that something that perhaps you need to go back and do as a team?

[Reveals own thinking and reasoning]

TL: Yeah, I think that taking that step back to look at what is our shared understanding of vocabulary because that certainly came out. Everyone just jumped ahead to the strategies and tools. There were a lot of different ideas brought to the table, but they weren't narrowed or focused enough. It was clear there were a few misconceptions and different ideas of what the strategies were or what was meant by certain terms as well. So, I guess building that shared understanding of what we're all talking about will help us develop a clearer sense of what our goals are for our inquiry spiral.

[Articulates the problem clearly with a solution now able to be developed]

SL: And that's something I notice in lots of inquiry teams is that everyone jumps to grabbing 'what's the fix' or 'what we need to change' without actually really spending that time looking at what is it actually that the students need to know and understand, how are we going to assess that, like what's our criteria around that and then what's some of the learning that we need to do as teachers to develop an assessment to find out where they fit, before they actually move to action. I've got a document here from a website to show what the inquiry team needs to know before moving to action. If you haven't done this preliminary work first, then it's hard to move forward as a team.

[*Uses an artefact to deepen learning at a relevant point*]

TL: I think that would be useful. We need to backtrack before we can go forward. It looks like this might help us get there.

[*Agreement on the problem as a basis for developing a solution*]

Acknowledge emotion and vulnerability

Many educators feel vulnerable when trying something new. Working with other professionals or students in new ways inevitably leads to feelings of uncertainty. Yet, reacting emotionally to uncertainty is often regarded as unprofessional. Research from the OECD (Dumont et al. 2010) and others has demonstrated that emotion is integral to cognition and learning. The work of Twyford et al. (2017) showed that when educators feel highly vulnerable, they do not have the cognitive resources to try new things, to learn from them or to try again when they do not work. They are also unlikely to ask others for help. Leaders who acknowledged these emotions, while still expecting change, had teachers who engaged more fully and became more willing to change their practice.

Compounding the problems around acknowledging emotion and vulnerability is that many leaders, unused to talking about emotions with others, feel highly vulnerable when they do so because of the newness of this territory and the potentially unpredictable reactions they are likely to encounter. For this reason, I have provided some prompts to start conversations in this difficult area, which have arisen from the work of Twyford et al. (2017). The following prompts can help leaders to probe emotions and model the behaviours they would like to see in their teams:

- Is there anything that you are not sure or uncertain about before we go on?
- I'm wondering if you have any 'what ifs' or concerns about what we've talked about?
- Is there anything I can do, you can do, or we can do that may help to remove some of these 'what ifs'?
- If you could change something to decrease these 'what ifs', what would that be?
- What do you think might happen if things don't work out as you hope?
- Can you tell me the sorts of things you are worrying about? Is there one thing you are most worried about?
- We don't often talk about emotion and professional learning. We don't know for sure how any new learning is going to go. How are you feeling about it at the moment? Is there anything going on for you?
- One of the ideas that I see that connects uncertainty and learning is the idea of vulnerability. Have you connected these ideas before? What do you think? How is that sitting with you?

For all of these prompts there is an assumption that a prior part of the conversation provides the rationale – so they do not become questions without reasons and leave the respondent wondering why they are being asked (see Chapter 2 on genuine and pseudo-inquiry).

💡 THINKING PROMPTS
- Am I avoiding acknowledging others' emotions?
- How do I feel about asking about how they are feeling?
- How might I respond?

In the following conversation, a senior school leader (SL) has asked to attend the next team meeting because the team leader (TL) has complained about the disengagement of the team on a number of occasions, but discussing these problems has not resolved any of the issues.

SL: You are looking a bit uncomfortable with the idea that I come to the meeting. I wanted to get a feeling for the team dynamics so we can work out what to do, but I have the impression you have some reservations about me being there?
   [*Acknowledges the non-verbal signs of emotion and probes neutrally*]

TL: Well, actually I do a little bit. It feels like this is happening quite quickly. I haven't had time to process all the information you have given me with these resources.

SL: So, tell me what's behind that? You've had the resources for a while, and we've talked several times about me coming to observe what's going on. I get the impression there is something more happening here.
   [*Probes for emotions without getting distracted*]

TL: Well, there's a difference between 'I'd like to see what's happening in your PLC' and 'I'm coming on Thursday'. And I'm like 'Oh, I don't know what I need to do for Thursday'. You know what I mean? Because I'm one of those people that likes to go off and plan, and I just felt like all of a sudden you are coming, and I haven't planned the meeting yet.

SL: It sounds like you are a bit unsure about me coming because you've had such short notice. Would it make any difference if we delayed it a week?
   [*Acknowledges the emotion and puts forward a possibility to reduce it without sacrificing the opportunity to progress PLC leaders' learning*]

TL: Mmm … I like to always show my best …

SL: Ok, we need to talk through what's underneath this because on one level you know the reason I'm coming is to work out the dynamics among the team, not for you to look your best at whatever …
   [*Probes what is underneath the surface emotion*]

TL: I suppose. I'm just one of those people that just wants to be getting it right and it's not going right. I'm really not sure about what I need to be doing.

SL: Would it help if we planned the meeting together, so that way I really understand what you are trying to achieve. I can observe the

team dynamics and we can meet immediately afterwards to figure out some ways to work towards solving the problems. Would that reduce your anxiety a bit?
[*Reduces uncertainty, which reduces vulnerability*]

TL: I kind of went into a bit of a panic. Planning it together would help – but I'll still be nervous.

SL: I know. When is a good time to plan it?

Plan and analyse deeper conversations

Planning, practising and analysing your conversations is just as important for the strategies in this chapter as it is for those in Chapter 2. It is only through practice and analysis that you will be able to keep focused on improvement in your conversations, particularly if you can do so with a colleague or someone with expertise in professional conversations.

As you become familiar with these deeper strategies in conversations that promote professional learning, your planning and analysis needs to include the aspects that you want to focus on for your own professional learning. For example, prior to the conversation you may want to think about how you could use the ladder of inference if you think the other person frames things differently from the way you do. Then during the conversation, you could draw the other person's ladder of inference together and follow up with an analysis by comparing your ladder of inference with theirs.

You may want to do the same with the theory of action template. The important issue is to be transparent about the process with the other person, check with them for accuracy, then reflect on the extent to which the use of the template promoted learning and adaptive expertise for both you and the person with whom you are having the conversation.

At this point, it may also be beneficial to revisit the planning and analysis templates provided for Chapter 2 in the supplementary digital resources (see p. 116) and personalise them by deleting the parts you found unnecessary and adding any new aspects covered in this chapter. Space is provided under each of the 5 prompts in the planning framework and under the 4 headings of the criteria for analysis for you to add extra material pertaining to this and the next chapter, 'Expert level'.

CHAPTER 4
Expert level

Introduction

This chapter picks up and elaborates on some of the strategies that were introduced earlier and the thinking behind them. The descriptions and the conversations go into greater depth. The strategies in this chapter are identified in Figure 4.1.

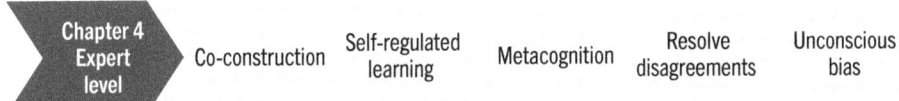

FIGURE 4.1 Features of conversations described in Chapter 4: Expert level

Many of the strategies described in this chapter, such as co-construction, promoting self-regulated learning and meta-cognition, are well recognised as high-impact strategies for student learning. The processes for professional and student learning have many similarities because they are about how all people learn (Bransford et al. 2000). This means that many of the conversational strategies are equally applicable to the learning of both students and those responsible for educating them.

In Chapter 1, the ideas of adaptive and routine expertise were presented. The conversational strategies in this book are focused on developing adaptive expertise, where educators develop new theoretical knowledge in ways that can be actioned, they use this knowledge responsively to meet the learning needs of the educators and students they are working with, and they seek feedback on the effectiveness of their efforts. At times, developing this kind of expertise challenges beliefs about leading, teaching and learning. Those with adaptive expertise are open to this challenge. While all the strategies described in this book contribute to the development of adaptive expertise, this chapter is particularly relevant.

The thinking and strategies illustrated in this chapter, however, may not be appropriate for all conversations. In some circumstances, particularly with a leader or teacher who is struggling in their role, more basic conversations may be more productive. If a teacher is unable to engage students sufficiently to manage their behaviour, for example, encouraging them to become more metacognitive is unlikely to be helpful. A team leader who needs basic skills in analysing evidence of student learning will probably not engage with the ideas of unconscious bias at this point in time. The 'level' of conversation and the strategies used become a matter for a leader's professional judgement.

Up to this point, the illustrated conversations have involved 2 participants only for practical reasons. The strategies, however, can all be used with groups. If the theory and reasoning underpinning them are understood at a sufficiently deep level, then the strategies can be transferred from the one-to-one context to group situations. As described previously, deep learning is transferrable learning (Pellegrino and Hilton 2012). If the strategies are seen as a series of techniques, without the underlying reasons understood, then transfer to group situations will be challenging. The final section in this chapter is designed to facilitate transfer by providing an illustrative example of how the same principles and strategies can be used to promote professional learning with groups of educators.

Co-construct conversations

The deepest professional learning conversations do not take a question/answer format, where someone with greater expertise asks the questions and the person(s) with less expertise answers them. Yet, this is the format of many of the conversations I have analysed. Much more effective is the sharing of thoughts and ideas, where one person builds on the other's contributions. Co-construction in this context involves working together to deepen thinking in ways that address the complex challenges the participants face. Each person makes a genuine contribution. One may have greater expertise in the area of focus, but the other is likely to have greater knowledge of their context and access to their own thinking about particular challenges and possibilities for addressing them. Do things make sense to them? Can they see how a specific approach might work for them in their context?

Many of the strategies identified in earlier parts of this book contribute to co-constructed conversations. They are usually jointly planned from the outset. The focus is agreed, with the kinds of evidence that might inform the focus decided together. The only questions asked are checking questions about understanding and agreement. In deeper conversations, even these questions disappear, as each participant contributes their ideas with an underlying assumption that if there is disagreement or limited understanding these issues will arise naturally as part of the conversation. As understanding and actionable knowledge is developed, the theories underpinning and reasons for that knowledge are elaborated and unpacked. Relationships involve significant challenge as each participant probes and unpacks developing ideas.

💡 THINKING PROMPT

- Does this conversation feel like I'm doing all the work, or are we thinking and puzzling things out together?

In a written transcript, co-construction often appears as if each person is talking over the other, but on closer inspection they are actually building on each other's ideas as each thinks out loud. Rather than interrupting one another, they are thinking together.

In the following example, a team leader is (TL) working with an early career teacher (T). They were puzzling over a child's lack of progress in reading in the junior school.

TL:	So, let's have a look at somewhere this student has re-read … so here they've re-read but haven't corrected it	
	[Looks for evidence to develop a diagnosis]	
T:	Here as well. Okay, so they're re-reading and … and they've got meaning and structure working …	
TL:	So, what's not working?	
	[Thinks out loud and reveals their own question about the evidence]	
T:	Visuals. I kind of knew that but so many of the kids rely on visuals I didn't want to draw too much attention to it.	
	[Reveals their own thinking]	
TL:	You're right. Yes … They're reading for meaning, to comprehend. But a lot of the time they're reading for meaning and maybe that's why they're re-reading, because they're thinking, 'Well, all this makes sense, but I know it doesn't look right'.	

        [Deepens the teacher's understanding]
T: So, I need to do something about the visual …
TL: Yes.
T: So probably tell them, 'Run your eyes through the whole word'. And, what's the other prompt that you said earlier was really good?
        [The teacher asks a question]
TL: Umm … We want them to make – what comes out of their mouth needs to match what's on the page. Visual cues.
        [Provides an answer]
T: But I'm worried they'll become dependent on the visuals and forget the meaning.
TL: So, you still want to keep that meaning as the pinnacle of your lesson. But for them …
        [Addresses the teacher's concern]
T: Because they're relying on meaning and structure, it is visuals. Yes. That's what's letting them down. I get what you're talking about now. Yes.
        [Demonstrates understanding of the strategy]

A potential comment on this transcript is that this early career teacher is able to articulate their thinking, but many others would have difficulty doing so. The counter evidence is that some leaders are more successful than others at helping teachers to do this, no matter who they are working with. They create this kind of co-construction with whomever they work with. It is more about giving the other person 'wait time' and encouraging them to think aloud to reveal their thinking, as the leader reveals theirs. In the same way that providing wait time for students to think through their responses is important, it is similarly important to provide wait time for teachers who need to think through new ideas and how to put them into practice. I have rephrased this in the prompt as 'thinking time'.

💡 THINKING PROMPT
- Am I giving the other person enough thinking time or do I rush in to fill the silences?

In the next example, the same team leader (TL) is working with another early career teacher (T) to help them to differentiate their mathematics instruction.

In an earlier part of the conversation, they had talked about the key concepts underpinning differentiation.

> TL: So, let's work out which kids are going to be able to do this task.
>
> T: Um, you know, I think it will engage … most of the class. Yes, I may need to differentiate for my lower students, but not like all of them, only a couple … [pauses]
> *[Team leader provides thinking time for teacher]*
>
> TL: Or maybe assist them with getting started [pauses]
> *[Provides suggestion and pauses for response]*
>
> T: And then they could go on and there would be time to work with the others. Some are doing it for 2-digit numbers and others are up to 3 digits …
> *[Picks up on the idea]*
>
> TL: It could be 220 or 30. That's a way of …
> *[Makes idea concrete]*
>
> T: Differentiating it.
>
> TL: So, let's look at …
>
> T: So, I think, like, the number talks. So, at the moment the lower group are using like 2 digits but then we're moving to 3. When we get to 3, I may need to differentiate for the lower kids, like instead of saying 345, I'll keep it as a 10 number. Maybe 340 or lower. And the number they are subtracting isn't such a big number as well.
> *[Teacher demonstrates they understand through a practical example]*
>
> TL: So, you could differentiate by using smaller and larger numbers for different groups.
> *[Confirms the teacher's thoughts]*

Promote self-regulated learning

The importance of fostering self-regulation for students is undisputed. Butler et al. (2017) define self-regulated learners as those who identify goals, problem-solve strategically, persist in the face of difficulty and engage in iterative feedback cycles. The same applies to professional learners. Self-regulated learning is fundamental to the development of adaptive expertise.

Self-regulated learning is often associated with cognition; what we know and how we think. However, it is more than this. It is also about self-regulating motivation and emotion. As noted in Chapter 3, cognition, motivation and emotion are interrelated and together impact on what is learned. Self-regulation also involves cycles of strategic action that include setting goals, planning, enacting strategies, monitoring and adjusting. This strategic element is fundamental to developing the self-efficacy and professional agency that is so fundamental to adaptive expertise.

Butler et al. (2017) remind us that self-regulation is not about working alone – instead, it is highly social. They suggest the term 'co-regulation' as more appropriate to describe how self-regulated learners navigate their social contexts and act strategically within them.

I have touched on several of these ideas in illustrative conversations in earlier chapters. Self-regulation is promoted by unpacking theories of practice; for example, when participants examine the consequences of particular practices and decide together what alternative actions (and the beliefs on which those actions are based) are most likely to achieve more desirable consequences.

Strategic action in professional learning situations is fostered by every educator, whether a leader or a teacher, when they identify and work towards specific professional learning goals. When using this book, for example, a professional learning goal may be to master some aspect of these professional conversations. Whenever changing practice is agreed to, conversations need to include statements and questions like:

> We've agreed on the changes you will make. What is the most important professional learning goal for you right now and how will you collect evidence to monitor if you are on the right track?

Deep learning in relation to self-regulation is, of course, promoted when the learner understands the reason for having a professional learning goal and the strategic importance of collecting evidence to monitor it.

💡 THINKING PROMPT
- Am I taking responsibility for this person's learning, or am I promoting self- and co-regulated learning where I am the support rather than the driver?

Acknowledging emotion and vulnerability and working together to manage feelings are part of developing self-regulation when things get difficult. If the person initiating a conversation manages these aspects unilaterally by 'reading' the other person's emotional state and making adjustments, such as cancelling meetings, then self-regulated learning is not promoted. Managing emotion in ways that promote self-regulated learning may look like the following:

- I see you are upset about what I have told you. I'd like to take a few minutes to figure out how we can make it work for you.
- You sound really nervous about me coming to observe you. How can we manage this jointly to take some of the anxiety away?

Develop self-awareness: metacognition

Sometimes, metacognition is considered to be part of self-regulation, or alternatively self-regulation is considered to be part of metacognition. Clearly, both are closely interrelated. Metacognition involves awareness of oneself and how one thinks and learns. It is reflected in the understanding individuals bring to activities about learning and about themselves as learners. Lucas and Claxton (2010) explain that it is essentially thinking about thinking. High levels of metacognition lead to highly reflective, intrinsically motivated educators, together with the teams in which they participate.

Metacognition is often confused with reflection. Reflection is an act of looking back in order to process and make sense of experiences. Metacognition is more about recognising patterns in one's activities, monitoring one's thinking and realising the need to do something different in the moment.

In the following example, a regional leader (RL) is working with a school principal (SP) to help them recognise and reduce the number of initiatives they have at the school and their tendency to create more and more. The principal realises that what they are doing is leading to exhausted middle managers and teachers.

SP: But I just can't help myself. I see so many opportunities and in my mind they are little adjustments. But then I find that the teachers think it's huge. And then there is another delegation to my office.

[Principal recognises and reflects on patterns in their own behaviour and the consequences]

RL: When you feel like you want to add more, what could you say to yourself that might be a prompt for you along the lines of, 'It's going to be too much. Stop.'

[Regional leader encourages principal to monitor their own thinking]

SP: Well, I'm aware of one thing that happens; I talk faster and faster because I kind of know I'm bombarding them when I say it, but I'm thinking, 'If I just slip it in, they might not notice'.

RL: If you find this happening, you could describe what you are thinking out loud as a cue for yourself and that will help others realise you are trying to stop. Something like, 'Here I go again!' It could become a bit of fun.

[Develops a metacognitive prompt]

The next conversation is between a senior school leader (SL) and an early career teacher (T). The teacher was experiencing a similar problem to that of the principal above, but in the teacher's case it was about teaching too many aspects of writing when they were modelling. In order to understand the issue in more depth, the school leader had co-taught a lesson with the teacher.

T: What I'm struggling with is just breaking it down to one learning intention to focus on in my model. I keep thinking, 'There's so much more to writing'. And when a student responds with something, I just want to go deeper – a bit more complex.

[Teacher reveals their thinking]

SL: Remember the other day when I was co-teaching with you, and we were talking about taking one step at a time. And I was modelling the writing and I turned to you and said …

[Models the metacognitive prompt]

T: [quoting the school leader] 'I could teach about that! It is so tempting, but I'm going to stay focused on my learning intention.'

[Articulates the metacognitive prompt modelled by the school leader]

SL: Exactly! That is the skill we have been talking about – metacognition – where you step back and look at what it is that you are thinking. You have got this other part of your brain that is saying, 'No, stop I am not going to do that'. It's not just what you say out loud.
[*Identifies the strategy as a metacognitive prompt*]
T: It's so hard.

Some other metacognitive prompts in conversations might be:

- You know how you learn best. What would be most helpful right now?
- I saw you stopped yourself from reacting when that happened. What were you thinking?
- Can you tell me what prompts you need for you to stop saying ... and to say the alternative we discussed instead?
- In this situation, how can you become aware of your thinking?
- Can you tell me how your thinking has shifted over this conversation and what this means for your practice?

💡 THINKING PROMPT
- Do I use these kinds of metacognitive prompts, or do I not even think about them?

Keep the main thing the main thing

Both the examples discussed in the previous section are about helping the principal and the teacher to respectively keep the main purpose of their joint work at the forefront of the conversation and not to get distracted by other possibilities. Distractions in professional learning conversations happen for many reasons, ranging from a lack of clarity about purpose to a preference by one person to deflect and distract from difficult issues. In the latter case, clarity about purpose can provide the context for challenging the distractions. For example, when someone keeps sliding into alternative topics, particularly when feeling challenged, one way to address this is to say something like:

I understood we were meeting about ... You keep bringing up [something different]. We can put that on the agenda for next time, but I think it's important to resolve [the original focus] first because ... Is that ok?

If distractions continue, it may be important to unpack why the person is appearing to distract by saying something like:

I understood we agreed to meet about ... You keep bringing up [something different]. I suggest we pause and unpack why you keep bringing this up. I'd like to know what is going on for you.

💡 THINKING PROMPT
- Do I sometimes feel frustrated that we never get to talk in any depth about important issues because we drift from topic to topic?

Adaptive expertise, however, requires that there is some flexibility in following through on the original purpose if issues arise throughout the conversation that are clearly more important to the other person. Under these circumstances, renegotiating the shift in focus makes it deliberate and helps to stop conversations drifting from one topic to another without progressing learning about any single aspect in sufficient depth to make a difference to leading, teaching and learning. In the following conversation, a regional leader (RL) was reviewing a 5-year plan with a school principal (SP) towards the end of the first year. Early in the conversation, it becomes clear that the principal's pending resignation is clearly of greater importance than the 5-year plan, although these are closely connected.

SP: So, we're in the first year of our 5-year plan. And when I reviewed things midway this year, we weren't nearly where I thought we would be. You know, I started the year all gung-ho ready to go but then we had the midyear review. We had some factions of little groups, and one staff member, who's new, was really pushing and questioning the ideas of PLCs and all of those things. They came from a single classroom structure and spoke to one of the school leaders and said, 'You know, I came here for autonomy. That's why I came here'. Which is what I've suspected all along, and they finally verbalised it.

RL: So, they thought a single classroom school and no PLCs would give them autonomy as opposed to the more shared practice in this school?

SP: Yes. And I suspect, they're not the only one who's come here with that in mind. So, midyear we had a little regroup and we started again, using the PLC website resources and the staff have done some of the matrix and are doing all that sort of stuff.

And then we also asked them to put their individual thoughts on post-it notes. What they individually wanted to say. The post-its were really low-level stuff. And I put on the table that I thought that we were cooperating not collaborating and the reasons why, and that there was still some trust to develop and how we were going to do all of that.

The reaction just made me want to give up. I'm feeling worn out. We were making progress and now it's all going backwards.

RL: This sounds like something we need to talk about. Is it just a 'bit down' or 'down for real'?

SP: 'Down for real' actually. I've got my resignation letter in my drawer. I'm not sure whether I'll send it in.

RL: Let's switch the agenda for this meeting.
[*Regional leader changes the focus of the conversation*]

Clearly, the issue of resignation and what was leading to it, was more important than the review.

Resolve disagreements

Although these conversations are about promoting professional learning, disagreements may still arise as a result of competing educational values, preferred ways to lead, or different beliefs about how students learn. Many of the strategies outlined in earlier chapters help to dissipate sources of disagreement before they arise and help to build trust and reduce the chance for disagreements to develop or escalate. These strategies include:

- developing a shared purpose for the conversation
- identifying beliefs about a particular situation
- using the ladder of inference
- unpacking theories of action
- using evidence 'to inform' an analysis rather than to 'prove a point'.

Mutual respect of different views, together with clarity and genuine inquiry in identifying them, are fundamental to resolving disagreements. When different views are mutually respected and identified, many disagreements evaporate, because disagreements arise as much from misunderstandings as fundamentally different opinions.

On the other hand, disagreements are likely to persist and escalate if one of the participants in a conversation believes they are right and that it is their job to persuade the other person of just how right they are. Inquiry becomes pseudo-inquiry. Persuasion trumps respect.

So where to start? A good place is to acknowledge the disagreement and clarify that the purpose of the continuing conversation is to explore the disagreement to see if there is any common ground. Often when leaders detect disagreement, they move the conversation on quickly to avoid potential unpleasantness, rather than slowing down and identifying the underpinning differences.

Mutual respect is promoted when each person is given the opportunity to state their point of view and the grounds for holding that point of view, with an expectation that the other person will listen and inquire into what they are unclear about. It also helps everyone to feel that they have been heard. Interrupting and talking over one another in these situations has the opposite effect. Careful summarising at each stage, with an emphasis on identifying the common ground, helps clarity. If common ground can be found, then it becomes the basis for moving forward. If it cannot be found, then it may be that all that can be achieved is to agree to disagree. If the differences have major implications, such as for the strategic direction of a school, then the disagreement clearly needs to be taken one step further. This step goes beyond the professional learning purpose of this book.

The touchstone for resolving disagreements should be the impact of each person's viewpoint or actions on student learning and wellbeing. Arguments about preferred pedagogical approaches should be adjudicated by impact on students, not whether one approach is preferred over another. There are, of course, many possible student outcomes that can be considered desirable and some educators will give priority to outcomes that others believe to be less important. A leader may be passionate about twenty-first century competencies, for example, but these competencies may appear very nebulous to a senior science or English faculty head whose students have shone on state assessments that do not assess these competencies. When each participant in the conversation respects the viewpoint of the other and sees these different viewpoints as competing theories rather than one being right and the other wrong, compromises that integrate both are more possible. In one example in Chapter 3 about rich tasks in numeracy, the team leader was more willing to consider pedagogical approaches that incorporated rich tasks when she could see how her concerns about direct teaching of numeracy strategies could be addressed.

I have not provided a specific example of a conversation here, because I have found that in high-quality conversations about professional learning that incorporate the strategies above, disagreements tend to dissipate.

Check unconscious bias and equity

Everyone has unconscious biases. They form the basis of how we understand the world around us. A bias is unconscious when we are unaware of it and it happens outside of our control. Unconscious biases are triggered automatically by our brains making quick assessments of people and situations. Our biases are influenced by our background, cultural environment and personal experience (Equality Challenge Unit 2013).

Biases become problematic when they lead to disadvantaging some groups of leaders, teachers, or students, while advantaging others. At the professional level, has someone won a promotion because they look and sound like us, so we can recognise their competence within our own frame of reference? Have they prepared their promotion application according to a set of unwritten rules? Are some staff allowed speaking time, while others are 'talked over'? Educators typically do not deliberately favour some over others and are shocked when this becomes evident to them.

The following statement is a quick check on one kind of common bias – what sense do you make of it?

> A father and son get in a car crash and are rushed to hospital. The father dies. The boy is taken to the operating room and the surgeon says, 'I can't operate on this boy because he's my son'.

If you struggled to make immediate sense of this statement, you are among the 50 to 70 per cent of people who do so. If it immediately made sense, this may mean you do not have unconscious biases towards gender and professionals, but it does not mean that other biases you may hold are not problematic.

For students, biases impact on equity. In a New Zealand study involving over 11,000 students, Meissel et al. (2017) were provided with teachers' end-of-year overall judgement of the students' writing achievement. The researchers then compared these teacher judgements with the same students' standardised scores on a writing sample. On average, for students with the same standardised score, the teachers judged girls to be better writers than the boys when making their overall judgements. The effect was compounded when boys were from ethnic minority groups. For these students with the same standardised score, European and Asian girls were judged by teachers to be much better writers than Māori boys or those from the Pacific Islands. This effect was evident irrespective of school size or the socioeconomic level of the community. When the findings were taken back to the teachers, they were shocked. No teacher deliberately downgraded a student's result. There are an increasing number of studies internationally demonstrating the same kind of bias in many different contexts.

Conversations to challenge such biases are highly fraught, but it is essential to have them if equity goals are to be realised. Challenges that come 'out of the blue' are likely to be met with defensiveness. It is more effective to create a climate where biases are acknowledged and routinely checked with positive endorsement when they are detected. At the professional level, a routine check may be along the lines of 'Who do we see as potential leaders in this school?' Then deliberately check gender, ethnicity and other relevant categories for potential bias. Another question might be to ask each member of staff about hidden barriers to achieving personal and organisational goals.

💡 THINKING PROMPTS

- Do we ever stop and think about our own biases and how they impact our actions?
- Do we talk within our organisations about possible unconscious biases and consider their impact?
- Do we know how to raise the issue? Is it safe in this school to do so?

It is probably safe to assume the existence of unconscious biases towards those student groups who do not typically achieve as well as others. In the New Zealand study, the bias disadvantaged those groups already achieving less well than others. This gap was greatly magnified in the teachers' judgements. Every conversation about these students needs to be accompanied by collective metacognitive prompts, such as:

- Do we unintentionally hold different expectations for different groups of students?
- Are we misjudging these students in any way?
- How can we check with them if we are creating barriers rather than opportunities?

Professional learning conversations in teams

All the strategies identified in one-to-one conversations can be used with teams, provided the leaders understand the principles and values underpinning them. Co-construction and keeping the main thing the main thing may translate into co-constructed agendas and not getting distracted by administration in a meeting planned for professional learning. Unpacking theories of practice can be collective as well as individual. Developing a shared pedagogy across a school means everyone being clear about the beliefs and values on which the pedagogy is based, with constant monitoring of consequences for the students to ensure the shared pedagogy is having the desired impact. Any process involving the analysis of student evidence involves interpreting the evidence by moving step-by-step up the ladder of inference. When evidence of student learning and wellbeing is analysed, it is quite possible that there are as many interpretations of that evidence as there are people in the room. Linking evidence of student learning to teaching practice is likely to involve multiple interpretations, with differences needing to be resolved.

Examples of group conversations are difficult to follow out of context, so I have provided an example of a structured professional learning process that incorporates many of the principles outlined in this and earlier chapters. It is called, 'Exploring puzzles of practice'. The process involves a group of teachers analysing evidence of student learning and the associated professional practice. Each teacher in the group takes turns presenting their students' work that is a puzzle to them. Teachers who have participated in this process consistently report it as respectful of their professional knowledge, while expanding, refining and often challenging it.

Exploring puzzles of practice

This team activity involves exploring 'puzzles of practice' through collaboratively discussing some form of written evidence of student work. In one meeting, there is usually time for only one or 2 teachers to present their work. Preparation involves making copies of one or more samples of the student's work for each team member and providing a brief summary of the task the student was to complete, together with the student's strengths and challenges in relation to the task. A 5-minute video of the teacher working with that student provides a richer picture. Leaders need expertise (or access to it) in both relevant pedagogical content knowledge and in leading conversations.

The protocol presented in Table 4.1 is a guide to examining and discussing the student work. Like all protocols, it could facilitate conversations, or it could limit them. Far more important than the protocol itself is to consider the underlying principles outlined in various parts of this book and to use them to promote professional learning through the analysis of evidence and practice. Timings are a guideline only, but each phase should not take longer than the suggested time.

TABLE 4.1 Protocols for examining student work in teams

Protocol phase	Guidance to participants	Rationale
1. Establish the purpose for the meeting (2 minutes)	Establish the professional learning purpose of the meeting and check understandings and agreement. [This step can be dropped after a few meetings.]	Establishing purpose provides clarity and 'keeps the main thing the main thing'.
2. Review previous week's focus (3 minutes)	The teacher(s) whose student work has been discussed in the previous meeting reports on whether the agreed actions have made a difference and describes the evidence.	Reviewing the previous week's focus promotes self-regulated learning and commitment to act on new knowledge, together with evidence of outcomes for student learning.
3. Describe the student work and the 'puzzle of practice' (10 minutes)	The teacher presenting the student's work describes the learning intention, the success criteria used to evaluate the work, and the aspect of the student's work that was puzzling for the teacher. A short video of the student working with the teacher links teaching to learning. Other teachers ask questions of clarification.	Presenting the work and the teaching helps to highlight these links. Clarification questions are accompanied by reasons, so they do not become pseudo-inquiry questions. (Pseudo-inquiry questions need to be challenged if they arise.)

Protocol phase	Guidance to participants	Rationale
4. Interpret the student work (7 minutes)	The teacher listens to the group as it tries to make sense of what the student was doing and why. The group should try to find as many different interpretations as possible and evaluate them against the evidence. Group members try to infer what the student was thinking, what they do or don't understand and how the student interpreted what they were supposed to do.	The process is essentially an interpretive one, so there are rarely simple answers. Deliberately moving up the ladder of inference reveals thinking and different theories of practice. Meanings are co-constructed. This provides an opportunity to notice and challenge unconscious bias.
5. Implications for teaching practice (7 minutes)	Based on the group's observations and interpretations, suggestions with reasons (presented as possible options) are linked to interpretations in Step 4. The suggestions are discussed with the teacher, who indicates how useful they find them. Leaders ensure suggestions are linked to theoretical constructs.	Suggestions linked to theoretical constructs promotes professional learning at a level that is sufficiently deep for transfer to practice. The requirement to provide reasons deepens the conversation.
6. Implications for teaching for the team (4 minutes)	All teachers make links to their students and puzzles of practice. They document their commitment to act in their own learning environments in a professional learning journal.	Linking to teachers' own learning environments promotes deep transferrable learning, actionable knowledge and commitment to act on it.
7. Implications for professional learning identified (5 minutes)	Any additional support that might be required for any of the group to act on the suggestions is identified, such as observing someone else, reading relevant information or having someone assist them when they try it out.	Those with adaptive expertise seek the support they need to improve.

Plan and analyse expert conversations

Planning and analysis at this expert level is essentially the same as planning for the other levels. Deliberate planning, practice and analysis of personal professional learning goals leads to improvement.

At this stage, it is particularly important to think about some specifics in the 'Anticipated knowledge, dispositions and vulnerabilities' section of your planning framework that relate to strategies in this chapter. For example, when thinking about the other person's commitment to moral purpose and curiosity, consider any issues related to unconscious bias that potentially impact on equity.

Also, when considering the other person's theories of practice related to teaching and leadership, bear in mind whether they tend to get distracted or if they are strong in 'keeping the main thing the main thing'. When undertaking the analysis of your conversation, carefully consider if you were successful in keeping them on-track in ways that respected their professionalism and if you have left them with strategies they can use in other situations.

A key focus at this expert level is to share responsibility for promoting learning through co-constructing conversations, promoting self-regulated learning and metacognition. These are all central to developing adaptive expertise. As a leader, the important questions become 'How much responsibility am I taking for this person's learning?' and 'Am I the support person or the driver?' These questions are relevant to both planning and analysing your conversations.

As with Chapter 3, it may be helpful to add anything new you have learned from this chapter to the planning framework and analysis criteria templates provided in the supplementary digital resources (see p. 116).

Lastly, an important motivator for anyone's learning is also to celebrate progress. Do this by returning to some of the recordings and transcripts of your earlier conversations and compare them with your current transcripts. If you have been practicing, you should see a deepening of your conversations as you have worked through the different chapters in this book.

CHAPTER 5
Observation and analysis of practice

Introduction

Throughout the earlier chapters in this book, many of the examples of conversations are supported by some evidence of practice or its impact on others. This chapter addresses conversations around more formal observations and a following analysis of practice. The analysis process is more commonly referred to as 'feedback', but I prefer to refer to it as the 'analysis of practice' to capture the idea of co-constructing an analysis of the observed practice using agreed criteria, from which to create new ways of doing things. Feedback implies a unidirectional flow of information from one person to another about an assessment of practice. This idea of a co-constructed analysis is more consistent with the learning focus of these professional conversations and the development of adaptive expertise. Figure 5.1 identifies the features of these practice analysis conversations.

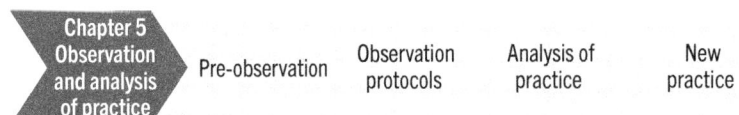

FIGURE 5.1 Features of conversations described in Chapter 5: Observation and analysis of practice

The analysis process and the stages outlined in this chapter are based on a 4-year research project I undertook in 200 schools, which demonstrated a strong impact on teacher learning and student literacy achievement (Timperley 2014). The participating teachers rated the approach as having a greater influence on their learning and practice than any other professional learning activity in which they had engaged.

Since that research was conducted, Twyford et al. (2017) found that formal observations and feedback often create strong negative emotions for many teachers, leading to feelings of vulnerability that affect their openness to learning. Part of the reason given by teachers for feeling so vulnerable was that they felt they had little control over what was observed and when. One of the features of the process I developed (Timperley 2014) is to give teachers agency over the focus of the observation and to frame it as a co-constructed joint analysis of practice, rather than a process that leads them to feel they are the passive recipient of someone else's feedback.

Observations do not need to be 'in-person'. In many situations, a video recording is often more effective because it ensures that both parties are watching the same interactions, with the person being observed becoming an active participant in the observation process, as if in real time. In addition, video recordings can be paused, reversed and discussed as a situation evolves. Video also allows the person being observed more time to reflect and prepare for the post-observation analysis conversation and gives them more control over what is shared, even to the point where they may delete one attempt and re-record what they want to discuss. This degree of control helps to reduce vulnerability and has no detrimental effect on learning. In fact, it provides opportunities for practice. Twyford (2016) found that, after some initial uncertainty, teachers preferred using videos to in-person observation.

The practice analysis process has 4 phases. In brief, the first is a pre-observation conversation. Its purpose is to unpack the context, develop criteria for effectiveness and make joint decisions about process. The second involves the observation itself, using the agreed criteria, and constructing a recording of what is occurring. The third involves a co-constructed analysis of the observed practice, focusing on the agreed criteria, and an assessment of its impact on the intended learners. For example, in a classroom situation, assessment of impact would focus on student learning. In a team meeting, this assessment would be focused on the extent to which the teachers learned what was intended. The fourth phase identifies possible new practices and ways the observed person would monitor them in terms of their effectiveness.

This process parallels that of formative assessment for students (James and Pollard 2011; Wiliam 2011). The person being observed has a learning goal, co-constructs success criteria with the observer, co-constructs an assessment of practice against the criteria and develops new goals for themselves as a result.

In the research on which the process is based (Timperley 2014), facilitators of teachers' professional learning found that the pre-observation conversations became longer and more powerful in shaping professional learning and practice, with the post observation analysis becoming shorter because shared understandings had already been established.

The next 4 sections of this chapter detail the phases of the practice analysis process. Each phase is illustrated with examples from 2 practice analysis conversations – one is between a school leader and a teacher about an observed lesson and the other involves a deputy principal working with a faculty leader. The transcripts from the deputy principal–faculty leader conversation show how the practice analysis process works when the focus is on developing leadership capability.

Phase 1: pre-observation conversation

This initial phase is often omitted or not given sufficient attention, yet it is fundamental to setting up a shared understanding of purpose, process and context for the observed practice. This kind of clarity reduces uncertainty and vulnerability (Twyford et al. 2017).

This first phase is also designed to deepen professional knowledge through the co-construction of criteria that will be used to analyse the observed practice and that will influence how the impact on outcomes is assessed. The observed practice may be in the form of a video recording. The key features of the pre-observation conversation, the rationale for them and links to strategies outlined in other chapters are identified in Table 5.1 (see p. 94). These features do not need to occur in the order listed. More important is to develop a shared understanding of each. A corresponding template repeating the main features of pre-observation conversations with a column for notes is also included in the supplementary digital resources (see p. 116).

Phase 1 features are illustrated in the pre-observation conversation between a school leader (SL) and a teacher (T) on page 95. The school leader is working with a teacher to model features of effective paragraphs to assist struggling students in the junior class in a secondary school. In this situation, the criteria for the teacher focused on effective modelling, with the outcomes for students being the quality of their paragraphs.

TABLE 5.1 Pre-observation conversation features and rationale

Pre-observation conversation features	Rationale
Develop purpose and process and logistics for the 4 parts of the conversations. Agree on the organisational issues (e.g. when the observation will occur or when the video will be recorded and the planning materials that need to be available).	Clarity reduces uncertainty (see Chapter 3).
Identify the specifics of the intended learning during the observed/recorded activity and how it is to be achieved.	For teachers, the learners are likely to be students. For leaders, the learners are likely to be other leaders or teachers. Evidence of impact on their learning and practice should be the purpose of the observed activity (see Chapter 2).
Identify how the observed person intends to promote others' learning.	This discussion of the promotion of others' learning develops understanding of and engagement in the reasons underpinning practice (see Chapter 3) and links leading/teaching actions to the intended learning.
Identify the impact of practice so far on the desired learning outcomes (i.e. what has been tried in the past).	This discussion of impact to date deepens understanding of the reasons underpinning current practice.
Identify ways to establish if the students and teachers involved in the learning activity are learning what is intended.	Identifying ways to check learning ensures the effectiveness of practice is assessed in terms of impact on learning and that evidence is collected (see Chapter 2).
Co-construct the observed person's professional learning goal.	Identifying the professional learning goal gives focus to the analysis of practice and promotes self-regulated learning (see Chapter 4).
Co-construct the criteria for effective practice in relation to the observed person's professional learning goal and the intended learning for the participants.	Discussing effective practice for both professional learning and learning of participants establishes theory-practice links, situating the specifics of practice in a theoretical framework of effectiveness (see Chapter 3). It also provides the basis for analysis following the observation.

SL: It's great we can have this conversation before I come into your classroom to observe, because I know observations can make some people nervous. I wanted to have the opportunity to discuss any of your concerns, or fears, and to be clear that this is about promoting your professional learning, not checking up on you or anything like that.

[Identifies purpose; acknowledges potential uncertainty and emotion]

T: Yes, I realise that.

SL: The idea is to work out the learning goals you have for your students and for yourself. Then after the observation, we'll have a look at how things went and what your next steps might be. Is this what you thought? Is there anything you want to raise at this point before I go into some details?

[Identifies overview of the process; checks for shared understanding]

T: I just wanted you to know that I've only just started on paragraph structure. We're not as far along as I wanted to be, but some students are really struggling.

SL: What would be most useful for you at this point? Do you want me to focus on the struggling students so we can work out together what's next for them? Or do you want me to focus on some other students and what they are learning?

[Identifies the students to focus on giving the teacher greater agency]

T: Actually, the struggling students would be good.

SL: Can you tell me who they are and what appears to be the problem?

[Seeks to identify the impact of practice so far on the desired learning outcomes]

T: [Identifies 5 students and outlines a general problem that they find it difficult to construct a paragraph with clear structure and internal cohesion.]

[Begins to identify the specifics of intended learning]

SL: That's really helpful. Can you tell me how you have tried to work with them in previous lessons and what you intended to do in this next observed lesson?

> [*Seeks to identify how the teacher intends to promote students' learning, including what has been tried in the past*]

T: I've tried giving oral and written feedback, but they don't seem to be able to revise their paragraphs. So, I thought I'd be more proactive this time and model constructing a paragraph using a list of key features and then to check their own work.

SL: Probably a good idea to go back to direct teaching rather than feedback because feedback is effective only if the student has a basic understanding of what they are learning. If they don't know it, teach it rather than give feedback.

> [*Links theory and practice; articulates the theoretical place of direct instruction and feedback*]

T: I hadn't thought about it like that, but it's the conclusion I'd come to.

SL: So, let's look at your professional goal – sounds like it is to model the structure of a paragraph in a way that these 5 students understand the features of a well-structured paragraph and can write a basic paragraph with these features, and assess their own work.

> [*Looks to establish if the students are learning what is intended*]

T: It might be more than we can get through in one lesson, but yes that's the basic idea.

SL: Yes, it probably is. But I want to pause a moment here and work out together some criteria for you around modelling. The outcome is that the students understand and can use the information. That's the outcome we want. In terms of observing what you do in your teaching, I was thinking that while you are modelling you are thinking aloud about how your paragraph illustrates the key features. Another criterion might be that you check the students' understanding of those links as you work through your model. Are these teaching process criteria making sense?

> [*Identifies the specifics of intended learning for students; co-constructs the criteria for effective practice in relation to the teacher's professional learning goal*]

T: Yes, they are.

SL: Are there any additional criteria you want to add?

T: Not at the moment.

SL: We might want to add some after the observation. Is there anything you have concerns about as we've talked?
[*Checks for possible uncertainty and vulnerability*]
T: Not at the moment. Are you just going to focus on those 5 students?
SL: Yes – if we can shift them, we can use the information to teach others. I'd like to talk to them during the lesson, so I get an idea about what they're understanding about paragraphs. I think I can be most useful to you if we have this information to add to our discussion. Is that ok?
[*Demonstrates ongoing transparency about the process so there are no surprises*]
T: Yes, that's fine.
SL: So, let's draw up an observation sheet that captures the criteria that I can use during the observation.

There can be greater challenges involved in establishing criteria for effectiveness in leadership situations, which are often more complex. For example, a team leader might want support from a senior leader to work with a group of teachers who are feeling challenged by the behaviour of some of their team because they distract from the learning purpose of the meeting. The criteria for the practice in this situation would focus on the extent to which the team leader is able to keep the group focused in ways that maintain a productive working relationship. These criteria can be thought of as the leadership practices designed to achieve the learning outcome of the team members. The impact on outcomes for the team may be the extent to which professional learning in the team enabled them to learn how to improve their practice.

The following example of a pre-observation conversation between a deputy principal (DP) and a faculty leader (FL) in a secondary school also illustrates the main features outlined in Table 5.1 (see p. 94). Earlier in the year, they had discussed the importance of developing a shared pedagogy around feedback among teachers in the faculty and how these shared understandings are better developed through collaboration rather than superficial participation in faculty meetings. They had agreed that the deputy principal would come to the faculty meeting the following day.

DP: Earlier in the year, we were talking about developing a shared approach to feedback across the faculty and this would be the focus of your faculty meeting tomorrow.

FL: Yes, I'd started to lose sight of it a bit, but we really need to come back to it. As a team that came together at the start of the year with quite different pedagogies and backgrounds, we've made a lot of progress. Now we can each speak to each other as well. I think people understand where there are differences, but I guess it's really the follow-through on feedback now.

[Identifies the impact of practice so far; identifies the focus in the faculty for the teachers' learning]

DP: So that I understand what you are trying to achieve tomorrow, is there a specific aspect of feedback you want to focus on?

[Makes this focus more specific]

FL: Yes. It's actually the feedforward. We did quite a lot on feedback but not so much on feedforward. I think we need to revisit what feedforward is really about, and how to make it concrete in their planning would help to make sure it happens.

DP: OK. So, you want the members of the faculty to understand the ideas around feedforward and include opportunities for feedforward in their planning?

[Summarises the learning focus for faculty staff]

FL: Yes. I've asked them to bring examples of feedforward they've given in the kids' work and told them we will be looking at their examples in terms of our discussion about high-quality feedforward. We'll go through that first.

[Identifies how they intend to promote staff learning]

DP: Now I just want to turn to your professional learning goal. Earlier, we were talking about the difference between participation and collaboration. And you've identified you like the idea of deepening collaboration among the staff in the faculty.

FL: [nods agreement]

DP: What I'd like to do now is to set up for tomorrow's meeting, to think about what you'd want to see in terms of collaboration as you are working to establish common processes around feedforward and planning. I guess what we want to come to is what do you think of as collaboration? What sorts of things – what do you think that means? I can tell you what I think it means. And maybe set up some criteria so we're both on the same page. When I'm in the meeting, what would I be looking for? What sorts of things would we see as being evidence of really good collaboration moving forward?

> [*Observes the faculty leader's professional learning goal established prior; signals the need to set up criteria for the observation*]

FL: So, I guess a shared voice, or that every person has a voice and a contribution to the discussion.

> [*Identifies first criterion (participation)*]

DP: Yes …

FL: But a willingness to challenge each other as well, so not – not just accepting what someone's got to say just because they've said it, but actually a willingness to ask questions and to challenge the validity of an idea. I guess they're the 2 big things. And it's interesting because I think they do challenge each other respectfully quite well. But the equal voice among the team can be an issue, which means that, even though that challenge might be there, Nur's response can sometimes dominate and therefore it hinders that open discourse. The other problem is they don't seem to put into practice what we've agreed. We do a lot of talking but not always a lot of action.

> [*Identifies second criterion (challenge); links the 2 criteria*]

DP: Let's summarise. So, the shared pedagogy around feedforward is genuinely shared and not just Nur's ideas. Respectful challenge is part of that, but also really developing that ownership of what they're going to go away and do. And they actually plan and do it. So, expecting that from them as well? And of course, we'll develop some strategies once I've got a sense of what Nur is doing if it continues to be a problem.

> [*Identifies a third criterion for collaboration (ownership); identifies a fourth criterion (planning for action)*]

FL: Yes. I'm most concerned about Nur.

DP: I want to capture the ideas on this paper here so we both know what I'll be focusing on. I've been listing what we have been talking about down this left-hand side. The first one here is participation. That shared voice and everyone has a voice. The next one is respectful challenge and then I've got ownership of the planning process around feedforward. The last one here is agreement about action. Is that what you want to focus on in relation to collaboration?

[Summarises the 4 criteria for collaboration]

FL: Yes.

DP: And on this paper, I've noted the learning of the faculty members you are trying to promote is to continue to develop a shared pedagogy for feedforward, the planning and follow-through. How does this sound? It feels like quite a lot to me. How does it feel to you?

[Summarises specifics of intended learning for faculty staff; checks for agreement and vulnerability]

FL: No, it's fine. It has to all come together if things are going to progress. And we've been working on this for a while now. It's not as if it is new.

DP: I'll make notes here when I'm in the meeting and we'll discuss them afterwards. Of course, you are welcome to call on me anytime during the meeting if that will help progress things. Although I'm observing, I can still participate.

[Is clear about the process; offers support to reduce vulnerability, but ensures the faculty leader controls the deputy principal's involvement]

Phase 2: protocols for observation/video recording

Trust is enhanced when the observer follows through on the agreed focus and notes observable behaviours in relation to this focus as far as is practical. Nothing on the observation schedule or notes taken should come as a surprise to the observed person. The last section included a pre-observation conversation between a school leader and teacher around junior school students struggling with paragraphs. The observation schedule following this conversation would look something like Figure 5.2.

In the pre-observation conversation between the deputy principal and the faculty leader, the observation protocol may look like Figure 5.3. Concepts such as ownership cannot, of course, be directly observed. Here is where the ladder of inference plays an important role (see Chapter 3). While noting behaviours

Process criteria and outcomes	Notes	
	Teacher	Students
Teaching process criteria		
Teacher thinks aloud about how their modelled paragraph illustrates key features		
Teacher checks students' understanding of the links between the key features and the model		
Outcomes for students		
Students demonstrate understanding of paragraph structure		
Students use features to construct their own paragraphs		
Students use features to self-assess paragraphs		

FIGURE 5.2 Sample observation protocol: classroom

Process criteria and outcomes	Notes
Criteria for professional learning goal	
1. Participation and shared voice	
2. Respectful challenge	
3. Ownership of planning process	
4. Agreement about action	
Intended learning outcomes for faculty members	
Shared understanding of pedagogy for feedforward	
Agreed planning framework inclusive of feedforward	

FIGURE 5.3 Sample observation protocol: faculty meeting

indicative of ownership, the observer needs to be aware that these behaviours may be interpreted differently by the person being observed.

Sample observation protocol templates for teacher and faculty observations are also included as templates in the supplementary digital resources (see p. 116).

Phase 3: co-constructed analysis of practice

The analysis discussion is shaped around the criteria established in the pre-observation conversation, whether an in-person observation or a video recording. This means that openings such as 'How do you think it went?' are replaced by statements like 'Let's revisit the criteria we established to analyse what was happening and how that worked for the students?' This focus on the criteria reduces many of the feelings that the observation is a personal evaluation and shifts the focus to how well the criteria for the task were met and the learning that was promoted. The deeper the discussion in the first phase, the deeper the analysis in this phase. The criteria themselves may need to be revisited if some aspects of the practice were not captured in the initial criteria. Features of this phase of the conversation are listed in Table 5.2. A corresponding template repeating the main features of co-constructed analysis with a column for notes is also included in the supplementary digital resources (see p. 116).

Phase 3 often becomes a series of iterations with phase 4, rather than a linear process. The conversation may oscillate between analysis of current practice related to one criterion and co-constructing alternatives, then return to the analysis focused on the next criterion. This occurs to some extent in the post-observation conversation around modelling paragraphs between the school leader (SL) and teacher (T). For this reason, there is a slight overlap in the transcripts used to illustrate phases 3 and 4 for that discussion.

> SL: Ok – so I wanted to follow up with what we both noticed during the lesson using the criteria we developed earlier on the observation sheet. You've had a chance to look through my notes. Has anything else occurred to you since then?
> *[Revisits the criteria for effective practice; providing notes in advance reduces feelings of vulnerability]*
> T: Well, it was obvious that 3 students [names] got it. They didn't have time to self-assess, but their paragraphs were structured according to the key features. They were heaps better. The other 2 showed

TABLE 5.2 Features of co-constructed analysis of practice and rationale

Co-constructed analysis of practice: features	Rationale
Revisit the criteria for effective practice in relation to the observed person's professional learning goal. The criteria may need to be revised in light of what took place.	The criteria build both theoretical and actionable knowledge (see Chapter 3). Revisions to the criteria deepen knowledge and link practice to theory.
Jointly analyse illustrative parts of the observed practice/video, using the criteria and the participants' responses as a guide. Both provide evidence and reasoning to support interpretations.	Illustrative parts focus on examples of the criteria to promote learning. Providing evidence and reasoning develops joint agreement of interpretations and conclusions (see the ladder of inference in Chapter 3).
Probe and examine what led the observed person to do what they did during the observation.	Provides exploration and understanding of the observed person's theory of practice so suggestions for change (phase 4) can be linked to current understandings and knowledge. Solution is linked to the problem.
Relate effectiveness to the extent to which participants' learning was enhanced.	Links practice to impact (see Chapter 2).

    some improvement but I don't think they really understand what a paragraph is. They had a topic sentence but then they kept bringing in other ideas.

    [School leader and teacher jointly analyse illustrative parts of the observed practice using students' responses as a guide; both provide evidence and reasoning to support interpretations]

SL: I think you've really identified what was happening for these 2. When I talked to them, they were trying to follow the details of the structure, but they didn't have a bigger picture idea that a paragraph has a single theme and that the individual sentences flesh out the theme in a way that has a consistent flow. They were trying to put too much irrelevant information in. Let's unpack what that might mean for your modelling and the paragraph features you were using.

> [*Relates effectiveness to the extent to which students' learning was enhanced; links teacher and learner voice on learning; deepens knowledge (start of phase 4)*]

In the leadership conversation between the deputy principal (DP) and faculty leader (FL), following the observation, the discussion revisited the first criterion of participation and shared voice:

DP: Thanks for letting me sit in. It was a real eye-opener for me just how much the discussion was initially dominated by Nur. So, let's revisit the first criterion we talked about, which was participation and shared voice.
> [*Brings the focus of the analysis to the first criterion*]

FL: Yes, you have to see it to believe it, which was why I've been so concerned. But Nur stopped dominating so much after a while. I have to admit, I was relieved.

DP: I think you managed that really skilfully and that's why Nur continued to contribute but didn't dominate so much. I've noted here, 'N asserts they always give feedforward'. You didn't interrupt but asked Nur to take a turn examining what high-quality feedforward looks like and to consider how Nur's stacked up, along with the others. That made it difficult for Nur to continue in an evidence-free way.
> [*Links leadership practice to Nur's responses; refers to description of evidence with some uncontentious interpretations further up the ladder of inference*]

FL: Yes. I've found that if we work through the features of something like feedforward and make Nur accountable by asking for classroom evidence, the self-praise stops.

DP: You seem to have this pretty much under control. But is there anything else in relation to this participation and shared voice you want to add or discuss?
> [*First criterion met; checks to make sure it has been covered from perspective of faculty leader*]

The faculty leader and deputy principal worked through and analysed each of the criteria and linked them to the faculty team's reactions, after which they agreed that participation and shared voice, together with respectful challenge and ownership of the process was largely achieved. However, they ran out of time in the faculty meeting to discuss anything about planning and action. This issue of time management during the meetings turned out to be a common occurrence. The conversation then turned to the extent to which the professional learning about feedforward was enhanced.

DP: So, getting these more collaborative processes in place, it seemed to me like they led to a shared understanding of an agreed pedagogy about feedforward. What's your take on that?
[Checks learning outcomes]

FL: They can talk the talk, but I'm not confident it will make any difference to their planning or teaching. This is the bit we get stuck on all the time. It always seems to get left off during the meeting and it wasn't the kind of outcome I wanted. It seems like no-one wants to commit to doing things differently.

DP: So, let's go into that a bit deeper because this is the hard bit.
[Acknowledges the difficulty and offers exploration of possibilities for new practice (phase 4)]

Phase 4: co-constructed new practice

In this phase, new ways of doing things to improve outcomes are developed jointly between the observer and the person being observed. Given the purpose of this conversation is intended to deepen theoretical knowledge of practice, as well as improve it, it is important to reference any suggestions and decisions about new practice to the theoretical constructs underpinning them. This may include supportive artefacts, readings or material on effective teaching and leading on reputable websites. The main features of this phase and the rationale underpinning them are listed in Table 5.3 (see p. 106). A corresponding template repeating the main features of co-constructed new practice with a column for notes is also included in the supplementary digital resources (see p. 116).

The final 2 features in Table 5.3 are often omitted from feedback conversations. They typically end by deciding on the new practices – a 'what will you do tomorrow' approach, which is more consistent with developing routine than adaptive expertise. In addition, changing practice does not necessarily lead

TABLE 5.3 Features of co-constructed new practice and rationale

Co-constructed new practice: features	Rationale
Co-construct new practice based on previous analysis and criteria for effectiveness.	Reference to criteria develops deep knowledge (Chapter 3). Co-construction respects the knowledge of both participants (Chapter 4).
Reasons for new practice are referenced to underpinning theoretical ideas.	Reference to theoretical ideas further deepens knowledge (Chapter 3).
Understanding/feasibility of new practice is checked.	Checking ensures the new knowledge is 'actionable' (Chapter 2).
The person observed identifies how they will know if the revised practice is more effective than the previous practice.	This step is central to self-regulated learning – the observed person needs to have ways to monitor their own effectiveness (Chapter 4).
A new professional learning goal is developed in light of the practice analysis.	Developing a new professional learning goal promotes self-regulated learning and ongoing improvement.

to improvement. For this reason, the promotion of strategic action within self-regulated learning that identifies specific ways to monitor effectiveness is essential (Butler et al. 2017).

The setting of new professional learning goals is also integral to formative assessment and self-regulated learning, as discussed in Chapter 4.

As indicated earlier, the conversation about modelling paragraph writing heads towards the construction of new practice when the school leader (SL) seeks to unpack the implications for the teacher (T).

> SL: I think you've really identified what was happening for these 2. When I talked to them, they were trying to follow the details of the structure, but they didn't have a bigger picture idea that a paragraph has a single theme and that the individual sentences flesh out the theme in a way that has a consistent flow. They were trying to put too much irrelevant information in. Let's unpack what that might mean for your modelling and the paragraph features you were using.

> [*Relates effectiveness to the extent to which students' learning was enhanced; links teacher and learner voice on learning; deepens knowledge (start of phase 4)*]

T: Well, the first issue is I didn't have the central idea of what constitutes a paragraph in the features that you mentioned – a single theme that every sentence elaborates with a flow. I've gone too much into the microstructure, topic sentence, elaboration, etc.

SL: Yes, I agree. And then when you model, you keep coming back to the big idea, as well as the specifics of the features. And maybe model that an idea has popped into your head, but then you check to see if it is central to the theme of the paragraph and leave it out if it isn't.

> [*Deepens knowledge; ensures new knowledge is actionable*]

T: Yes, I think I can see what was going on for them. I'd like to try that out next lesson.

SL: And maybe work out some ways to find out if these 2 students are getting it. It may also help consolidate the others' understanding. Let me know how you go.
Is there any new professional learning goal that comes to mind as a result of this conversation?

> [*Ensures the teacher has ways to know if their revised practice is more effective than the previous practice*]

T: I've just been thinking while we were talking, that maybe the bigger picture is something I leave out in other areas and that I focus too much on the details without ensuring the students have the big ideas to frame the details. I'd like to think about this.

> [*Begins to identify a new professional learning goal*]

SL: Let's talk further about this when you have had time to check out if this an issue for you more generally, or just relates to this context.

Phase 4 is also illustrated in the new approaches and professional learning goals that were jointly established by the deputy principal and faculty leader in their post-observation conversation around the faculty team meeting. After revisiting the criteria for effective practice and discussing the extent to which professional learning had been enhanced, they went on to unpack their respective hunches about why the faculty team had difficulty turning their talk into action.

Together, they decided the team did not know how to do so and decided that it was important to ensure meeting time was devoted to joint planning of action. They discussed how the faculty leader could support this transfer of knowledge to practice, the evidence they would use to evaluate if this was occurring, and new professional learning goals for themselves.

💡 THINKING PROMPTS

Many people ask for conversation starters and examples when starting out on the journey of practice analysis conversations. It is difficult to develop generic examples that do not sound stilted and out of context. What is more important is that your conversation is guided by some key ideas. These include:

- Ensure throughout your pre-observation conversation that you are both on the same page about what the process is all about.
- Keep professional learning values to the fore – do not use the process as an 'in' to deal with competence issues.
- Think of the process as a joint inquiry into the teacher or leader's practice and the beliefs underpinning them.
- Think of the parallels between formative assessment or assessment for learning and this practice analysis process and you will get the process right.
- Keep checking if the teacher or leader understands and is able to put into action any suggestions you make.
- Remember it is the teacher or leader, not you, who needs the tools and skills to monitor the effectiveness of their changes in practice if they are to become self-regulated learners.

Observation and analysis: further thoughts

This 4-phase protocol may appear to be time consuming with its pre and post-observation conversations. Those involved in the research behind this protocol (Timperley 2014), however, indicated that time was saved by reducing the number of observations, increasing their effectiveness and following them with quick check-ins about changes in practice and outcomes with those the observer is responsible for.

All the processes and strategies engaged in the earlier chapters are applicable to observation and analysis of practice. For example, being clear about the learning purpose of the observation and practice analysis, carefully moving up the ladder of inference from describing the practices observed and the participants' responses, making inferences and drawing conclusions. These processes are as relevant in these conversations as in any other. Drawing a theory of practice diagram may help to clarify beliefs and consequences. Prompting metacognition in ways that allow the other person to become aware of their own thinking and using self-prompts to help them monitor how they think and act in particular situations may interrupt habitual reactions. Particularly relevant is promoting self-regulated learning so the person observed is able to monitor the impact of changes to their practice in the future.

CHAPTER 6
Bringing it all together

The purpose of this book is to guide and illustrate the kinds of professional conversations that develop adaptive expertise through promoting and deepening professional learning. Professional conversations form the oil that connects people throughout an organisation and strongly influence the development of organisational cultures, together with the expertise developed within them.

Adaptive expertise is needed to address the complex challenges faced by all educators in our schools, regions and states. The increasing diversity of students means traditional ways of doing things are unlikely to meet the challenges inherent in the rapidly changing educational landscape.

Sound routines and the associated expertise are essential to well-functioning schools. They provide educators with efficient ways of doing things and students with a sense of order and certainty. On their own, however, they do not address the growing complexity faced by today's educators. More is now demanded of educators, and this is best addressed through the development of adaptive expertise.

Those with adaptive expertise have professional conversations with the following qualities:

- They help leaders and teachers think and act evaluatively about their impact on student outcomes to understand who is benefitting from their educational experience and who is not.
- They seek to develop deep knowledge as they grapple with how to make more of a difference for all students.
- They promote metacognitive thinking about biases and beliefs and how these unintentionally influence action and outcomes.
- They encourage collaboration because diversity of views is valued.

- They develop responsiveness to all learners to ensure they are benefitting from their educational experiences.
- They promote thinking systemically, keeping both the 'big picture' in mind and ensuring the direction of travel is towards creating this picture.

My work with educators, from beginning teachers to senior policymakers, has demonstrated that once those involved understand the difference between routine and adaptive expertise, they readily embrace the relevant mindsets and skills. The transcripts throughout this book are all based on real conversations and illustrate how to develop adaptive expertise in leaders and teachers at all levels of our education systems.

As mentioned previously, although most of the conversations in the book are between 2 people, the strategies outlined also apply to working collaboratively in groups. Many of the educators with whom I have worked, have indicated that their teams come to function very differently when they lead using these same strategies. It is still important to use genuine inquiry and engage the team's current beliefs, knowledge and skills about learning, teaching and leadership. Knowledge is deepened through unpacking the theory–practice links, with reasons provided for questions posed. Acknowledging emotion and vulnerability and promoting self-regulated learning encourages everyone to engage.

There are well-researched educational practices that are likely to be more effective in promoting student learning, inclusion and equity than others. I have written previously with colleagues that to be ignorant of such practices, or not to use them, is the equivalent of malpractice (Timperley et al. 2014). The process of professional learning about these educational practices and how to put them into action, however, is not about 'telling' other educators what to do. Rather, it means engaging their current knowledge and beliefs around a particular student-related challenge, figuring out together what the new practice might look like in that educator's context and why it might address that particular challenge. Most importantly, it involves working out ways to monitor if new ways of doing things are having the intended impact on student learning and wellbeing. The emphasis shifts from the correct way to implement something, to ensuring it is implemented in ways that actually benefit students and understanding the reasons why. Deep inquiry becomes a way of being.

The other approach to professional conversations I frequently encounter is a bit like the opposite of 'telling'. The main strategy is to ask questions. This approach arose as a reaction to the managerialism that developed in many educational jurisdictions in the late 1990s (Leat et al. 2012; Murray et al. 2009). The questions are designed to encourage reflection and the reasons for asking particular questions are not disclosed. There is no intention to present new knowledge directly, but rather to keep one's own views private; presenting them can be seen as equivalent to managerialist control. This approach respects and engages the views of teachers but is unlikely to create new knowledge or promote collaborative problem-solving.

The conversations described in this book are focused on addressing the complex challenges faced by all educators collaboratively, whatever their position. They engage all participants' beliefs, assumptions and biases because these are fundamental to how educators think about their responsibilities and how they enact them. These conversations unpack the complexity of educators' practice contexts to work out how to be responsive in-the-moment, drawing on deep knowledge of effective educational practice. The conversations help to keep in mind both the 'big picture' for improvement, while ensuring the direction of travel is towards shared goals. The type of discussions presented in this book do not provide absolutes and definitive answers. Instead, they offer genuine, deep inquiry into what is happening for learners and what educators need to know and do to promote an optimal educational experience for all students.

Learning how to have these types of conversations is like all deep learning: iterative, challenging and highly rewarding. It forms the essence of the metacognitive attribute of adaptive expertise. During these conversations, leaders find they are mentally juggling the following:

- understanding the context of the other person, together with their beliefs and knowledge
- checking the other person's engagement and interest in developing relevant knowledge and skills and whether any of it is making sense
- checking their impact on the other person, including their level of discomfort or emotion
- monitoring their own thinking and whether they are revealing it in ways that invite genuine inquiry rather coming across as 'Just do as I say'
- monitoring whether they are promoting adaptive or routine expertise
- genuinely engaging with the complexity of the issue at hand.

If this feels hard, then it is. However, most of the educational leaders I have worked with have demonstrated their ability to do this because the very nature of education means they are constantly engaging with complexity in their work. As in all skill development, it takes practice. The suggestions for practice in the book, supported by the templates and other material in the supplementary digital resources are designed to promote and deepen learning. All these suggestions are structured around the experiences of educators who have engaged in this work across many different education systems.

Learning is motivated by the learner's desire to know, not someone else's desire to tell them what they should learn (Timperley 2011). Despite this, some of the educators with whom I have worked have found it very difficult to present their views as possibilities to discuss, as opposed to withholding them or presenting them as a given that should be adopted by the other person. This takes practice, analysis and reflection on the conversation, with additional attempts for further analysis. This practice and reflection process is the iterative part.

Another skill many find challenging is the development of evaluative thinking, where all the participants in the conversation work together to design ways to collect evidence of impact on the learning and wellbeing of students. The focus is often on what to do, rather than evaluating the impact of that action. Students are best served by educators who monitor their impact on learning and wellbeing and become responsive to the evidence.

A third skill many of those I have worked with find challenging is to give reasons when asking questions. Asking questions of students is engrained in teaching practice. However, when shifting to professional learning situations that are designed to develop adaptive expertise, this practice needs to include giving the reasons for asking particular questions. The reasons allow the other person to understand why the person asking the question thinks this question is important and to develop a deeper insight into the thinking behind the question. Sometimes reasons are omitted because the person asking the question already has the desired answer in mind and hopes the other person will come up with the same answer without having to disclose it. More often, it occurs from a genuine desire to know something, such as what happened in a particular context. By not disclosing the reason for wanting to know, however, the questions are more likely to develop routine than adaptive expertise.

Like any challenging learning situation, the process involves having a go, getting some parts right and some parts wrong, taking risks and showing vulnerability by sharing with others that you are a learner in this work. Most of all, it involves being metacognitive as you develop your own adaptive expertise along with those with whom you are working.

Whatever challenges you experience in your own professional conversations, learning is best promoted when you engage in formative assessment processes (James and Pollard 2011; Wiliam 2011). This means developing criteria that are meaningful to you in your context, collecting evidence of current practice, using the criteria to identify a goal for improved practice and working towards closing any gaps that become apparent. The processes outlined in the book, supported by the supplementary digital resources, are designed to support you to do this as you deepen your learning, develop high levels of adaptive expertise, and increase your impact on student learning and wellbeing.

Supplementary digital resources

The supplementary templates and other materials mentioned throughout this book can be accessed at https://ambapress.com.au/products/leading-professional-conversations or via the QR code at the bottom of this page. The resources can be printed and utilised to support your professional conversations, particularly in the planning and analysis phases.

Resources provided include:

- Planning framework for professional conversations: template
- Criteria for conversation analysis: template
- Reflection for identifying the development of adaptive expertise: template
- Ladder of inference with prompt questions and ladder of inference: template
- Theory of action: template
- Pre-observation conversation: template
- Sample observation protocols (classroom and faculty)
- Co-constructed analysis of practice: template
- Co-constructed new practice: template.

References

Argyris C (1982) *Reasoning, learning and action*, Jossey Bass, San Francisco.

Bransford J, Brown A, Cocking R (eds) (2000) *How people learn: brain, mind, experience and school*, National Academy Press, Washington DC.

Bryk AS, Schneider BL (2002) *Trust in schools: A core resource for improvement*, Russell Sage Foundation Publications, New York.

Butler D, Schnellert L, Perry N (2017) *Developing self-regulated learners*, Pearson, Toronto.

Cochran-Smith M, Ell F, Ludlow L, Grudnoff L, Aitken G (2014) 'The challenge and promise of complexity theory for teacher education research', *Teachers College Record* (1970), 116(5):1–38.

Dumont H, Istance D, Benavides F (eds) (2010) *The nature of learning: using research to inspire practice – practitioner guide*, Centre for Educational Research and Innovation, OECD, accessed 11 August 2023. http://www.oecd.org/edu/ceri/50300814.pdf

Earl L, Timperley H (2016) *Embedding evaluative thinking as an essential component of successful innovation,* Seminar series 257, Centre for Strategic Education, Melbourne.

Elmore R (2004) *School reform from the inside out: policy, practice and performance*, Harvard Education Press, Cambridge, MA.

Equality Challenge Unit (2013) *Unconscious bias and higher education*, Equality Challenge Unit, London, accessed 22 September 2023. https://diversity.caltech.edu/documents/19785/unconscious-bias-and-higher-education-compressed.pdf

Goddard RD, Salloum SJ, Berebitsky D (2009) 'Trust as a mediator of the relationships between poverty, racial composition, and academic achievement: evidence from Michigan's public elementary schools', *Educational Administration Quarterly*, 45(2):292–311.

Hatano G, Inagaki K (1986) 'Two courses of expertise', in Stevenson HAH, Hakuta K (eds) *Child development and education in Japan*, Freeman, New York.

Heifetz RA (2010) 'Adaptive work', *The Journal of Kansas Leadership Center*, Spring 2010:72–77.

Heifetz RA, Grashow A, Linsky M (2009) *The practice of adaptive leadership: tools and tactics for changing your organization and the world*, Harvard Business Press.

James M, Pollard A (2011) 'TLRP's ten principles for effective pedagogy: rationale, development, evidence, argument and impact', *Special Issue: Principles for Effective Pedagogy: International responses to evidence from the UK's Teaching and Learning Research Program Research Papers in Education*, 26–36.

Leat D, Lofthouse R, Towler C (2012) 'Improving coaching by and for school teachers', in Fletcher SJ, Mullen CA (eds) *The Sage handbook of mentoring and coaching in education*, Sage, London.

Le Fevre D, Robinson V, Sinnema C (2018) 'Genuine inquiry: widely espoused yet rarely enacted', *Educational Management, Administration and Leadership*, 43(6), 883–899.

Le Fevre D, Timperley H, Twyford K, Ell F (2020) *Leading powerful professional learning: responding to complexity with adaptive expertise*, Corwin and Learning Forward, Thousand Oaks, California.

Lencioni P (2002) *The five dysfunctions as a team*, Barnes and Noble Press, Wheaton, Illinois.

Lucas B, Claxton G (2010) *New kinds of smart: how the science of learnable intelligence is changing education*, Open University Press, Berkshire, England.

Margolis J, Strom K (2020) 'Assessing the success of teacher leadership: the case for asking new questions', *Professional Development in Education*, 46(4):607–621.

Meissel K, Meyer F, Yao E, Rubie-Davies C (2017) 'Subjectivity of teacher judgments: exploring student characteristics that influence teacher judgments of student ability', *Teaching and Teacher Education*, 65:48–60.

Murray S, Ma X, Mazur J (2009) 'Effects of peer coaching on teachers' collaborative interactions and students' mathematics achievement', *Journal of Educational Research* 102(3), 203–212.

Opfer VD, Pedder D (2011) 'Conceptualizing teacher professional learning', *Review of Educational Research*, 81(3):376–407.

Pellegrino J, Hilton M (2012) *Education for life and work: developing transferrable knowledge and skills in the 21st century*, National Research Council, Washington DC.

Robinson VMJ, Lloyd A, Rowe KJ (2008) 'The impact of leadership on student outcomes: an analysis of the differential effects of leadership type', *Educational Administration Quarterly*, 44(5):635–74.

Shaked H, Schechter C (2020) 'Systems thinking leadership: new explorations for school improvement', *Management in Education*, 34(3):107–114.

Snyder S (2013) *The simple, the complicated, and the complex: educational reform through the lens of complexity theory*, OECD Education Working Papers, No. 96, OECD Publishing.

Timperley H (2011) *Realizing the power of professional learning*, Open University Press, Berkshire, England.

Timperley H (2014) 'Developing teacher effectiveness through professional conversations', in Tan O (ed) *International perspectives on policy and practice for building new teacher competencies*, Cengage Publishing, Singapore.

Timperley H (2015) *Professional conversations and improvement-focused feedback*, AITSL, Melbourne, accessed 9 August 2023. https://www.aitsl.edu.au/docs/default-source/default-document-library/professional-conversations-literature-review-oct-2015.pdf?sfvrsn=fc2ec3c_0

Timperley H, Ell F, Le Fevre D, Twyford K (2020) *Leading professional learning: practical strategies for impact in schools*, ACER Press, Melbourne.

Timperley H, Kaser L, Halbert J (2014) *A framework for transforming learning in schools: innovation and the spiral of inquiry*, Seminar Series 234, Centre for Strategic Education, Melbourne.

Timperley H, Robertson J (2011) *Leadership and learning*, Sage, London.

Timperley H, Twyford K (2021) 'Adaptive expertise in educational leadership: embracing complexity in leading today's schools', *Australian Educational Leadership*, 44(1):8–12.

Tschannen-Moran M (2001) 'Collaboration and the need for trust', *Journal of Educational Administration*, 39(4):308.

Twyford KM (2016) *Risk or resistance: understanding teachers' perceptions of risk in professional learning* [thesis], The University of Auckland, accessed 11 August 2023. http://hdl.handle.net/2292/29983

Twyford K, Le Fevre D, Timperley H (2017) 'The influence of risk and uncertainty of teachers' responses to professional learning and development', *Journal of Professional Capital and community*, 2:86–100.

Wiliam D (2011) 'What is assessment for learning', *Studies in Educational Evaluation*, 37(1):3–14.

www.ingramcontent.com/pod-product-compliance
Lightning Source LLC
Chambersburg PA
CBHW061127070526
44584CB00033B/4240